Edited by Gill Varley & Alex Sewter

The Gap Pack range includes:

★ **The Australia & New Zealand Gap Pack**
★ **Work & Travel Europe Gap Pack**
★ **Work & Travel Canada Gap Pack**
★ **The Careers Gap Pack**

Published by Gapwork Ltd
    60 Green Road
       Meanwood
       Leeds
       LS6 4JP

    info@gapwork.com
       www.gapwork.com

First edition 2003

Work and Travel USA Gap Pack

Edited by Gill Varley & Alex Sewter
With thanks to Daniel Weir, Elina Vartto & Kathleen Repper

Copyright © Gapwork 2003

ISBN 0954043391

Layout design by Gill Varley
Cover design by Anthony Barker
Front cover image reproduced courtesy of California Travel and Tourism Commission (copyright Robert Holmes)
Back cover images reproduced courtesy of San Francisco Convention & Visitors Bureau, Hawaii Visitors & Convention Bureau and Colorado Tourism Office
Printed by Active Print Media Ltd

# read this first!

★     How do you use your Gap Pack? Well, you can read it obviously - but there's much more to it than that! It's no ordinary guidebook. The USA Gap Pack includes general info about taking a gap year in the US but it also has heaps of info about each destination (we've picked 21 to keep you going), as well as everything else you'll need to make the most of your working holiday.

★     The first section of the pack contains general info about different kinds of jobs you can do in the USA, whether it's working as a camp counsellor, au pair, at a ski resort or in a bar. We've also included information about volunteering, placements, internships and studying.

★     Leading on from this is our travel section. This is an opportunity for you to get an insight into how specialist companies can turn your working holiday into the trip of a lifetime. Whether it's information on insurance, booking accommodation or getting your travel kit together, the host companies in this section are the experts.

★     Next comes the destinations section with work and travel tips for some of the USA's top cities. Here you'll find listings of accommodation, potential employers and things to do, as well as who to go to if you need help.

★     Towards the end of the book you'll find the web directory - pages of top internet sites that will help you research and plan your trip properly.

★     Finally there is a backpackers diary - a template to help you keep the details of your journey, the places you go and the people you meet - and address book, notes and personal details section.

★     Don't forget to visit our website at...

    www.gapwork.com
    for more top travel tips.

# contents

## Work & Travel USA

## Destinations

## Resources

# introduction

Do you feel like you already know the United States of America even if you haven't been there? Let's face it, American culture is everywhere we turn. Your view of the US might come from what you see in films and on the news, or from the McDonalds and Starbucks that spring up in your town centre, by the soft drinks you consume and the music you listen to. America has sold itself, its image and its products more successfully than any other country in the world. You'll either love it or hate it.

But there's much more to the States than corporate America, Hollywood or even George W Bush would have you believe. It's hard to comprehend just how diverse the country is. From New Yorkers and Native Americans, Hawaiians and African-Americans to San Franciscans and Alaskans, the variety of cultures and ethnic groups is incredible. The country is a fantastic hotchpotch of communities, many with different languages and dialects, food, music and art.

With 50 states (plus the District of Columbia, home of the capital) and over 280 million people, the number of places to visit, people to meet, and jobs and career opportunities available is mind-boggling, and far too large to cover comprehensively in a book this size. So we've given you a taste of what we think are some of the best places to live and work in the US.

Inside the USA Gap Pack you'll find loads of great advice on every aspect of making your working holiday or gap year a success, including travel contacts, accommodation info, visa advice and listings of potential employers on a city-by-city basis. And we've got some cool tips straight from the experts on how to prepare before you go and how to stay safe once you're there.

So whether you fancy hiking and skiing in the Rockies or dodging rattlesnakes in the deserts of Nevada, chilling on the beach in Hawaii or taking in a Broadway show in New York, watching great live Blues in St Louis or paying homage to The King at Graceland, we hope the USA Gap Pack will help to inspire you to get out there and experience it all for yourself.

# map

## usa

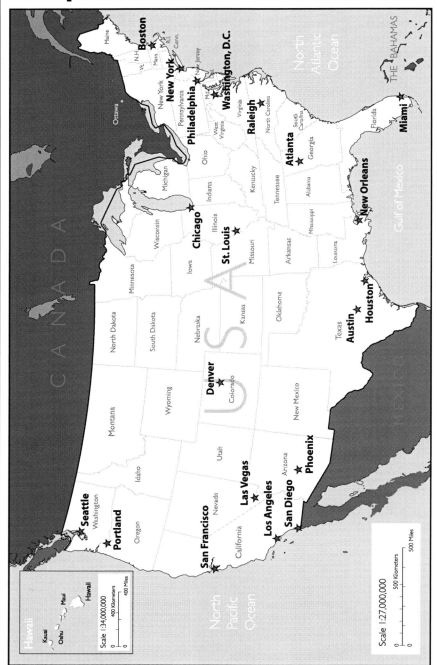

## Work introduction

Millions of people have travelled to the US in search of work over the past couple of hundred years and the lure of the American dream and the American dollar is as strong as ever. But finding legal work in the USA can be daunting and laborious without some kind of sensible, no-nonsense independent help. That's where your USA Gap Pack comes in! We've gathered together the most up-to-date information and tried to explain the options in the most straightforward way possible.

This first part of the book is split into the following sections...

- ☑ Sponsoring agencies
- ☑ Paid work
- ☑ Internships
- ☑ Placements
- ☑ Volunteering
- ☑ Studying
- ☑ Visas

Don't forget that further on in the USA Gap Pack you'll find more work contacts within each city. We've focused on bar work, hotel work, office work and some language schools to get you started.

So just read on and you'll get all the information, names, addresses and contact details you need to help you to organise your working holiday in the US.

image copyright: Robert Holmes/CalTour

## Sponsoring agencies

Before you can start planning any paid work, you need to be aware of America's awkward visa situation. The reality is that you really need to get a sponsoring agency, like BUNAC, to do it for you.

To work for most of the employers listed in this book, you will need to have the appropriate work visa. The most common is the J-1 visa. There are two different types of the J-1 visa. The US Government's Work & Travel Program allows you to work temporarily in the US in guest service positions. The Camp Counsellor visa allows you to work at a summer camp as a camp counsellor (obviously!). We've listed the qualifications for these visas in our more detailed visa section on page 27. There is also the H-category visa for temporary work that requires you to have a formal and specific offer of work from an American employer, and the F-category visa for students.

## Remember:

☑     After the tragic events of September 11th 2001 in New York, US authorities are scrutinising all types of visas that allow foreigners into the USA. As a result of this, visa eligibility criteria is subject to change, so check www.unitedstatesvisas.gov or speak to a sponsoring agency like the ones listed below to get the latest visa updates.

★     **BUNAC's 'Work America'** programme will guide you through the whole work and travel process. You get a J-1 visa, allowing you to work legally in US, booked on a BUNAC return flight and the Work America Job Directory and Handbook. You also get met in the USA, your first night's accommodation, arrival orientation, a travel guide and an interest free loan to help you pay for your flight if you need it.

      You must be at least 18 and a current full-time student on a degree level course.

      www.bunac.org

★     **The Council on International Educational Exchange (CIEE)**
Offers up to 4 months summer work in the US with 30 days to travel afterwards, and will do all the legwork for you – they'll help you to get a visa, and to get seasonal work anywhere in the US. Get more info from...

      www.councilexchanges.org.uk

# sponsoring agencies

★ **Alliances Abroad** – With their 'Work and Travel USA' programme you'll be placed in a pre-screened position and generally supported throughout your stay – helped with finding your feet, getting housing etc. Also offers Work Abroad, Teach Abroad and Volunteer Abroad programmes.

⬠ www.alliancesabroad.com

## Other sponsoring agencies for J-1 work & travel visa...

★ **American Work Experience**
⬠ www.aweusa.com

★ **Apex USA**
⬠ www.apexusa.org

★ **Cultural Homestay International**
⬠ www.chinet.org

★ **Interexchange**
⬠ www.interexchange.org

★ **Work Experience USA**
⬠ www.campcounselors.com/WEUSA/why_do_weusa_s.html

## Sponsoring agencies for J-1 camp counsellor visa...

★ **American Work Experience**
⬠ www.aweusa.com

★ **BUNAC**
⬠ www.bunac.org

★ **Camp America**
⬠ www.campamerica.co.uk

★ **Camp Counselors USA**
⬠ www.campcounselors.com

★ **Cultural Homestay International**
⬠ www.chinet.org

★ **International Camp Counsellor Program - YMCA**
⬠ www.ymcaiccp.org

★ **International Counsellor Exchange Program**
⬠ www.international-counselors.org                more overleaf >

# sponsoring agencies

usa

★ **Interexchange**
www.interexchange.org

These agencies may also be able to help you obtain a J-1 if you want to work as support staff in a camp.

## Remember:

☑ If you've only got a tourist visa, you'll probably be thrown out of the country if you're caught doing any kind of paid work.

📂 **Case study**

**Amy Adams talks about the practicalities of her Council Exchange trip to New York.**

"There I was, a finalist who watched far too much 'Sex and the City' and wanted an exciting after-graduation plan to tell various aunties, hairdressers and tutors about. But once I'd told everyone I needed to think about how I was going to even get there!

So the research began. I found BUNAC and Council Exchanges offered what I was looking for. They're authorised to give temporary visas to students, or those within a year of graduating, and will book your flights, apply for your visa, provide a welcome meeting at your destination and an emergency contact throughout your stay. They won't organise a specific job for you though.

I chose the 'Work and Travel USA' option with Council Exchanges which meant I could work for 4 months and then travel around America for another month (I guess the clue's in the name!).

So I pitched up in New York with no job, no work experience and no accommodation. It was a bit nerve wracking but the Council had organised two nights accommodation in a hostel. And after some help at the Council's Welcome Meeting, I soon found a perfect little apartment in Brooklyn that I shared with two Americans. It also meant I had an immediate social life!

With the help of my flatmate, I arranged some work experience on a magazine. My next priority was finding a paid job - New York is not a cheap place to live (no surprise). So I marched around the city in July heat filling out endless applications. My persistence eventually paid off and I found a hostessing job in a Chelsea restaurant.

Like many before, I really fell for New York but, after four months, I was ready to see a bit more of America. I organised my month travelling while I was in New York, booking Greyhound coaches and Bluejet flights to fit in as much as possible. I got to travel down the east coast to Miami and on to New Orleans.

My time in New York City was truly memorable – I really experienced life as a New Yorker. And, if you can make in there, you can make it anywhere (sorry, I had to get it in somewhere). I might not have been flouncing around in Manolo Blahniks but I certainly learned to walk taller."

## Paid work

On a J-1 visa, you can do any kind of work in America. But the nature of the programme means that as a student you are likely to be looking for the sort of temporary work that doesn't need you to be fully qualified or very experienced.

American cities offer plenty of opportunities for paid work with temping agencies or major employers. If you have good office skills then use them to earn some cash while you are in the city. If you have worked in a bar before you can pick up bar work much more easily in cities than you can in the mountain resorts, where everyone is after the same job. Retail work is also easy to find in the cities, particularly in the run up to Christmas.

In each destination within the USA Gap Pack we cover the following types of work...

☑       Bar & restaurant work
☑       Hotel work
☑       Temp agencies for office work

We concentrate on these types of work simply because they are the areas that are most likely to require your skills!

# paid work

## BUNAC

Getting the necessary paperwork to work legally in the USA can be a real headache if you try and do it yourself. So why not save yourself the trouble and let the professionals sort you out an organised placement, and take the worry out of working and travelling abroad?

One of the most well known of these is BUNAC, who run a number of different projects across the US. BUNAC is a non-profit organisation that arranges work and travel programmes for students and young people to various countries, and is the most popular choice for anyone looking for a hassle-free and unforgettable work and travel experience.

**BUNAC** offer a number of great organised schemes...

★     **BUNAC's Work America** programme is open to anyone over 18 who is a full-time student, and gives you the chance to live and work in the USA for the summer, with time to travel afterwards. You can do virtually any job you want, while gaining great experience of living in the USA.

★     **Summer Camp USA** is a fantastic opportunity to work as a camp counsellor in one of the many summer camps for young people across the US. It can be hard work but is a very rewarding way to spend your time in the USA, and BUNAC's programme also allows you time to travel afterwards. It's open to students and non-students between 18 and 35 who have worked with children and who are available from early June to mid August. You get at least $795 or $855 (over 21) in-hand total salary. The programme cost includes flight, food and lodgings.

★     **Kitchen and Maintenance Programme (KAMP)**, is for students who want to experience summer camp life but don't want to work directly with children. This placement includes a J-1 visa, free food and accommodation and an in-hand total salary of $1200. There's also the option to travel around the States for up to six-weeks after camp. You must be at least 18 and a current full time student.

★     **BUNAC's Overseas Practical Training Programme (OPT)** provides the opportunity to spend between 3 and 18 months getting training and experience in career or study related areas. In-job training is provided in areas from business and commerce to management, arts and education. Training is well structured and organised specifically to provide practical experience within the workplace and fit with the theoretical knowledge that students have developed while studying.

work & travel

# paid work

## Au pair work

The only legal way to go to the USA as a nanny is through a sponsoring agency. For more information try...

★ **Au Pair in America**
Au Pair in America is run by the American Institute for Foreign Study and send over 4,000 au pairs each year.
 37 Queen's Gate, London, SW7 5HR
☎ 020 7581 7322
🕸 www.aupairinamerica.co.uk

★ **Au Pair USA**
You must be between 18 and 26 years old and have at least 200 hours of infant care experience to qualify for placement in a family with children under two years of age. It costs $500 to join the program but this is refunded at the end of your stay. Everything else is paid for including flights, training and medical insurance.
🕸 www.aupairusa.ws

**Other agencies to try...**

★ **Almondsbury Au Pair and Nanny Agency**
At the moment they can only place UK nannies in the USA.
🖰 damien@aupair-agency.com
🕸 www.aupair-agency.com

★ **The Nanny Bureau**
Helps recruit nannies, au pairs, babysitters, mothers helps and maternity nurses in America.
🖰 info@thenannybureau.co.uk
🕸 www.thenannybureau.co.uk

★ **Sunny Au Pairs**
They are not a US designated au pair agency so they don't provide travel or J-1 visas. They can, however, organise a family homestay of up to 6 months with a B2 (tourist/visitor) visa.
🖰 support@sunnyaupairs.com
🕸 www.sunnyaupairs.com

# paid work

## Ski work

There are some big ski resorts in the US which are a massive draw for tourists from all over the world.

The kind of jobs available during the ski season include lift operators, janitors, bar and restaurant staff, guest services, equipment rental and repair, day care, ticket checking, parking attendants, cashiers, retail staff, room attendants and of course ski and snowboard instructors.

Most positions require you to have some experience in the relevant field – whether it's just customer services or catering. If you want to work as a ski or snowboard instructor, you will need to have the relevant qualifications.

As an employee of one of the big ski resorts you can expect to be on low pay and living in shared accommodation. However, you can also expect a discount on ski passes, subsidised accommodation and food, as well as an active social life! So if you are there for the love of the snow, rather than the need to earn lots of money you'll be fine.

## Ski work with a tour operator

Instead of heading off into the great unknown of America with nothing but a work visa and your skis in hand, you could apply for a job with a tour operator before you leave the UK. The benefits of getting work this way is that you get your accommodation, transport, ski pass, uniform and wages all included in the package. Ideally you should speak a second language, German or French is especially useful. A number of British package holiday operators have employment opportunities in their American resorts during the winter:

★ **TUI** own Crystal Holidays, Thomson Ski and Simply Ski. For their North America resorts they employ staff from reps, to kitchen staff and nannies. Crystal Holidays alone employ over 1000 staff in their resorts overseas. The season runs from November to April, and you will have to commit to working the full season.

 www.crystalholidays.co.uk

 www.shgjobs.co.uk

# paid work

★ **Inghams** is another big UK based ski package holiday operator with work at Aleyska, Big Mountain, Breckenridge, Jackson Hole, Killington, Park City, Stow and Vail. The minimum age for resort reps and managers is 23.

🕸 www.inghams.co.uk

★ **First Choice Ski** include training for applicants interested in positions as resort reps at Breckenridge and Winter Park. A resort rep is basically a customer service role, involving taking guests to and from the airport, sorting out room bookings and distributing ski passes. Being a rep is a tough job, not for anyone who thinks they'll be spending the winter bumming around on the slopes!

🕸 www.first-choice.com

★ **Skiworld Ltd** offers a wide range of seasonal employment opportunities during the winter, with approximately 26 positions of varying responsibility from Chalet Host to Resort Manager. The main recruitment period for winter positions is from June to October and staff must be able to commit for the whole winter period from mid November to April.

✉ Overseas Personnel Department, Skiworld House, 3 Vencourt Place, London, W6 9NU

☎ 0870 420 5912

🖱 recruitment@skiworld.ltd.uk

🕸 www.skiworld.ltd.uk

Also try...

★ **Free Radicals -** Independent ski recruitment specialists. As well as ski instructors and ski technicians, they also help recruit drivers, chefs, nannies, resort managers and chalet helpers.

🖱 application@freeradicals.co.uk

🕸 www.freeradicals.co.uk

★ **Cool Works -** A web site for finding 'Jobs in Great Places', features thousands of seasonal jobs at ski resorts in the Sierras, Rockies, Cascades and White Mountains. Also features employers in national parks, summer resorts, cruise lines, ranches and camps.

🕸 www.coolworks.com

★ **GoSki!** Coverage of over 700 resorts in the USA.

🕸 www.goski.com

# paid work

## Other work in ski resorts

During both winter and summer you can find work in large resorts. When the snow goes around April time, the resorts simply change tack and offer golf facilities, fishing, canoeing, sailing, windsurfing, scuba diving, hiking - anything in fact, that involves people being outdoors and enjoying the beautiful scenery.

Whether you are a trained canoeing instructor, have hotel reception experience, or simply want to wait tables or work in a shop, these resorts have plenty of opportunities.

The following are just a few resorts actively recruiting for the winter and summer season...

★ **Alyeska Resort -** Offers varied job opportunities and employee benefits including an all-mountain season pass.
Alyeska Resort Human Resources, PO Box 249, Girdwood, AK 99587
hr@alyeskaresort.com
www.alyeskaresort.com

★ **Big Mountain Resort -** Don't always accept overseas applications so check out their website.
PO Box 1400, Whitefish, Montana 59937
800 858 3930
bigmtn@bigmtn.com
www.bigmtn.com

★ **Northstar-at-Tahoe -** A winter and summer resort by Lake Tahoe in the Sierra Nevada Mountain - downhill skiing and snowboarding, terrain parks and a nordic ski centre.
PO Box 129, Truckee, California 96160
530 562 1010
info@skinorthstar.com
www.skinorthstar.com

★ **Park City Mountain Resort -** All year round resort near to Salt Lake City.
pcinfo@pcski.com
www.parkcitymountain.com

# paid work

★ **Vail Resorts -** One of the most popular ski destination in the United States with more than 1.5 million skier visits last year.

🖱 info@vailresorts.com

🕸 www.vailresorts.com

✎ **Note:**

If any of the ski resorts need summer staff, they will be described as "all season" or "four season" destinations.

image copyright: BUNAC

# internships

## Internships

✎ **Note:**
An 'internship' is the US term for a period of practical work experience.

You can only do a work experience programme with an organisation like BUNAC that can issue the DS-2019 form, which you need in order to then apply for a J-1 visa. If the program you're doing has training, teaching or research, or paid employment of some kind included, then you're allowed to do this work on a J-1 visa.

★ **BUNAC's Overseas Practical Training Programme (OPT) -**
The YMCA of Greater New York provides the sponsorship that lets you get a J-1 visa for this vocational business programme. The placement lasts for 3 to 18 months, and you can gain real practical experience of working in a real office environment. The placement will give you skills and training in an area that is closely linked to your area of study or your career.

⬠ www.bunac.org

★ **Council on International Educational Exchange (CIEE)** also provide an Internship USA Programme which means that you can work and learn on the job with a US employer for anything up to 18 months – its very vocational and has to be connected to your area of study or your future career. Find out more at...

⬠ www.councilexchanges.org.uk

★ **Cultural Cube** offers 12 to 18 month internships in hospitality and business training for students, graduates and professionals.

⬠ www.culturalcube.co.uk

★ **The International Association for the Exchange of Students for Technical Experience (IAESTE)** offers degree level students the opportunity to get work experience in America. Your degree should be in science, engineering, technology, applied arts or related fields. There are some placements available for language students interested in teaching English abroad. You can apply for the scheme in November, and then go on the placement in the following summer. The IASTE scheme is cost effective, in that you don't have to pay to go on it, but you will need to pay for your flights and insurance. Some universities offer financial assistance for these kind of exchanges.

⬠ www.iaeste.org

★ **Mountbatten Internship Programme** - If you fancy working in an office in New York for a year, then the Mountbatten Internship Programme could be for you. You'll get a Certificate in International Business at the end, and some fantastic experience to put on your CV. For more information go to...

www.mountbatten.org

image copyright: BUNAC

# placements

## Placements

A few companies offer paid work placements in the USA. You pay them to set the placement up, and they will arrange transport and accommodation.

★     **USA Placement** is a service for graduates and young professional people who want to work in the US for up to 18 months on the J-1 visa. They will help to put you in contact with a potential employer in the US, negotiate training for you, help with finding accommodation and getting a J-1 visa.

     www.internshipusa.org

Some organisations offer work placements for people interested in working in the agricultural industry in America. The advantage of these companies is that they sort out visas and placements for you, and provide back up while you are away.

★     **The International Agricultural Exchange** organises exchanges between the UK and the USA for people who are interested in farming. Usually applicants come from a farming background or have studied agriculture.

     www.agriventure.com

★     **Stablemate** arrange agricultural and equestrian placements to America.

     info@iepuk.com

     www.iepuk.com

## Volunteering

With an organisation like GAP Activity Projects, you pay them to organise your placement, accommodation and visas. They also provide back-up and support while you are away.

**For other companies offering volunteering placements in the USA keep an eye on our website...**

❀ **www.gapwork.com**

★ **Gap Activity Projects** provides a variety of volunteering projects in the USA, from caring for children and adults with disabilities to conservation placements.

☎ 0118 959 4914

🖱 volunteer@gap.org.uk

🕸 www.gap.org.uk

★ **Earthwatch** could get you directly involved in scientific field research. Each year it supports more than 130 expeditions in 45 countries, including the United States, sending approx 4,000 people into the field to work with leading scientists. As a volunteer you would collect data and work as an expedition member.

🕸 www.earthwatch.org

There are also charities that offer conservation orientated holidays rather than placements...

★ **The British Trust of Conservation Volunteers (BTCV)** provides volunteering holidays in places from Albany to the White Mountains. BCTV organises practical conservation projects for volunteers both in the UK and around 20 countries worldwide.

☎ 01491 821600

🖱 information@btcv.org.uk

🕸 www.btcv.org

Alternatively you can volunteer with a charity while you are in the USA. There are plenty of volunteer networks to research. See our web directory in the back of this book for relevant links.

# volunteering

 **Case study**

**Amberlee Foote talks about her decision to go to the US on a gap year, volunteering at the Chesapeake Bay Foundation.**

"I knew when I was 16 years old that I wanted to take a gap year. For me there would be no way I could cope with going into another three years of education. I have wanted to go to America for as long as I can remember. There was just something about the country that amazed me and, after searching the internet, GAP Activity Projects seemed the best choice as it had placements all over America and it also wasn't as expensive as a lot of other organisations.

Since I had studied biology and geography for my 'A' levels, I was offered the chance to be a 'guinea pig' on a new placement that had just been set up. GAP partnered up with an organisation called the Chesapeake Bay Foundation, a group whose motto is to 'Save the Bay'. The placement gave me the chance to intern for six months at one of CBF's education centres, which happened to be on islands in the middle of the Chesapeake Bay. They run education programs for three days where volunteers come and stay and get to learn how to protect the watershed and experience green living and life as a waterman. These trips included getting up at sunrise and setting crab pots for dinner, scraping for soft crab and other bay wildlife, going marsh mucking and getting completely dirty from head to toe in the saltwater marshes that surround most of the islands. This sounded like a dream - I love the water and being outdoors and to be able to combine that with teaching was the perfect placement.

So I have been living on Smith Island, one of the last inhabited islands in the bay, in a small town called Tylerton. Tylerton has a population of about 60 people, one small store and a church and the only mode of transport is golf carts! The Bay Foundation owns two houses that you share for the three days. It is the only education centre out of the four that is in the middle of the community so I am one of the lucky few that get to be part of this unique fishing town and the people that live there.

I have learnt so much from this experience. It has amazed me - not just about the Chesapeake Bay and the lessons that we teach - but how to live in a more environmentally aware way (and that I can survive without having a shower for three weeks!) I have also learnt a lot about me - I have learnt how to live away from home and am now an expert at using the washing machine (my mum will be so pleased!). This year has given me the biggest confidence boost in so many different ways and I feel that I am now more focused and ready for what ever lies ahead at university."

**work & travel**

## Studying

Surprise, surprise - applying to study in the United States isn't a simple process either. The best thing you can do is contact the closest US Overseas Educational Advising Office when you are making your plans. The Advising Office has a lot of information and can also help with things like financial planning, admissions procedures and visa requirements. Advisors work directly with the consular officials who approve visas.

★ **Overseas Educational Advising Centers (OSEACs)** provides contact information and links to each Advising Office around the world.
**OSEAS-Europe**
🕸 www.bibl.u-szeged.hu/oseas/europe.html
**OSEAS-Oceania**
🕸 www.bibl.u-szeged.hu/oseas_adsec/oceania.htm

★ **The Fulbright Commission** provides information on educational exchanges for school children, undergraduates and postgraduates, as well as scholarships for postgraduates, lecturers and people who want to do research.
☎ 020 7404 6994
🖱 education@fulbright.co.uk
🕸 www.fulbright.co.uk

★ **The Council on International Educational Exchange (CIEE)** promotes periods of study abroad for teachers, upper secondary school and university students.
🕸 www.ciee.org

★ **British Universities Transatlantic Exchange Association (BUTEX)**, as the name suggests, promotes study exchange between universities and colleges in the UK and North America. It represents over 80 higher education institutions in the UK with active transatlantic links and interests – most of them have individual exchange arrangements with North American universities and colleges
🕸 www.butex.ac.uk

# studying

Contact the following organisations to find out more about studying in America...

★ **The American Consortium of Universities -** Consists of five higher ed institutions and INTERLINK language centres.
✉ 1717 Washington Avenue, Golden, CO 80401
☎ 303 278 8337

★ **US Network for Education Information (USNEI)**
✉ National Library of Education, 400 Maryland Avenue, SW Washington, DC 20202-5523
☎ 800 424 1616
🖱 usnei@ed.gov

★ **Websites**
🕸 www.embark.com
🕸 www.studyusa.com
🕸 www.worldstudent.com

## Visas

Getting a visa on your own is a real hassle, and organisations such as BUNAC will help you through the application process – this is strongly recommended unless you have a firm offer of a job from an American employer before you go, who is prepared to vouch for you and do the necessary paperwork at their end. Immigration laws into the US are understandably tougher since September 11th, and the way that immigration law works (even for tourists) is that the official checking your visa application or passport has to presume that you are actually an immigrant. It is up to you to prove that you only want to stay in the US temporarily, and that you will definitely be going home at the end of your trip!

## The different sorts of visas:

### 1. The visitor visa
This is the most straightforward type of visa to get. Applicants for visitor visas from certain countries, including the UK and Ireland, can apply under the visa waiver programme. This means that your entry to the USA is more straightforward. You are not allowed to work on a visitor visa.

### 2. "J" category visas
This sort of visa is for those visiting the USA on an exchange trip. In theory it is to promote educational and cultural exchanges. In practice the J1 visa has been the best way of combining work and travel in the USA if you are a student. However, post September 11th, all visa regulations and eligibility have been tightened up, and you should check www.unitedstatesvisas.gov or speak to a sponsoring agency such as BUNAC to clarify the latest criteria for J1 visas.

### 3. "F" an "M" category visas
The "F" category visa is for those wanting to study an academic subject in America. The "M" category is for those wishing to study a non-academic or vocational subject. If you are offered a place by an American educational institution, you have to apply for an "F" or "M" category visa at your nearest American embassy or consulate. You will need to show evidence of enough funds to cover at least your first year of study on an academic course. For a vocational course you will need to show evidence of funds to cover all your costs throughout your entire stay.

# visas

### 4. "H" Category visas

The H-2A visa is for people wishing to work in America as temporary or seasonal workers in agriculture. The H-2B visa is for those wishing to work on a temporary or seasonal basis in a non-agricultural sector. These are only issued if you are offered a job in the US by an employer who has completed the correct paperwork at their end and has proven that they can't find any American citizen who can do the job instead. This is the kind of visa you'll need if you want to do any kind of work, permanent or temporary that isn't an organised program or exchange. If you want to get paid work in a ski resort or pick fruit for a few weeks, you'll need an H category visa, unless it's a recognised, organised programme.

### ✎ Note:

One area that the US Department of Immigration may be tightening up on is that all applicants for all these types of visas will need to have a definite job offer before they get their visa approved. Use the contacts in this book to get that job offer!

## How long can I work in the US?

☑ J-1 visa programmes vary in length, from a few months to a year and a half at most.

☑ H-category working visas allow you to stay anything from 18 months to 3 years, depending on what kind of visa you get.

Whether you're getting a J-1 visa for an exchange programme or an H-category visa for a pre-arranged job in the US, you're going to have to head to London at some point for a meeting with US Immigration. Contact details for the Embassy are listed below. A good starting for all things visa-related is the USA Immigration Services website...

 www.unitedstatesvisas.gov

## Embassies

For more info on work permits for British and Irish students contact the relevant embassy...

**London**
- ✉ 24 Grosvenor Square, London, W1A 1AE
- ☎ 020 7499 9000

**Dublin**
- ✉ 42 Elgin Road, Dublin 4
- ☎ 00 353 6688777

**Belfast** - US Consulate General, Belfast
- ✉ Queen's House, 14 Queen Street, Belfast, BT1 6EQ
- ☎ 028 9032 8239

**Edinburgh** - US Consulate General, Edinburgh
- ✉ Consulate General, 3 Regent Terrace, Edinburgh, EH7 5BW
- ☎ 0131 556 8315

**Cardiff** - American Embassy Welsh Affairs Office, Cardiff
- ☎ 029 2078 6633

image copyright: Robert Holmes/CalTour

# travelling

So, after finding out how you go about getting your work permit or visa, and what jobs you can do, you need to get some travel essentials sorted. Who better to help you do this than the experts?

In this section we help you to...

☑ Get your kit off (in the nicest possible way) and sort out what you are taking.

☑ Make sure you know about travel safety issues (sounds boring but it's not - it could make the difference between a trip of a lifetime or a holiday from hell).

☑ Cover yourself properly with an insurance policy.

☑ Book accommodation in advance to avoid a Mary and Joseph situation.

☑ Find out about getting there.

☑ Find out about getting around once you've got there.

☑ Use our communications pages to stay in touch.

☑ Keep track of your precious dollars in the money section.

☑ And know who to call if it all goes wrong.

So read on, enjoy! Got itchy feet yet? You obviously haven't read enough. And if you have any questions at this stage why not email us...

info@gapwork.com

image copyright: Robert Holmes/CalTour

# get your kit off

One of the most common questions asked by people thinking of going backpacking is - "what do I need to take?"

## Buying a rucksack

Your first concern should be a rucksack. Two things are important when choosing your rucksack: the first is fit, and the second is capacity.

The fit of the rucksack is vital because you are very likely to be carrying it for a lot of the time. Wandering round a hot city trying to find a hostel with a 60-litre pack straining at your shoulders is not a good way to start your trip.

Only buy a rucksack after you have tried it on (with weight in it). You are most likely to be buying a rucksack with an internally built frame, as these are good for comfort, flexibility and balance. Frameless rucksacks are more likely to be used for daypacks or climbing and other activities where flexibility is required. Rucksacks with external frames are an older design and are most appropriate for very heavy loads that need to be piled high on the back.

When you are trying on your rucksack, all the weight should be on your hips rather than on your shoulders. You should feel the weight being carried around the small of your back. This is where your natural centre of balance is.

A problem that some internal framed rucksacks have is that the surface that is against your back can prevent air circulation. This means that you'll have a hot, sweaty back - not what you need when trekking through a desert or some chilly mountains! Make sure that any parts of the rucksack that will be in contact with your skin are made of breathable, open cell foam. This should assist air circulation.

Size does matter. Too big and you'll be tempted to pack your entire life into it before you go. Too small and you'll just end up buying a bigger rucksack later on in your travels. For a long journey expect to need a good 60-litre rucksack.

Some manufacturers have designed rucksacks especially for women. These are shorter in the back, slightly narrower and have different hip and belt adjustment straps. Another development is the travel pack, a kind of cross between a rucksack and a holdall. It looks like a rucksack, but has a zip down it and adjustable straps so you can carry it like a case if you need to. These tend to be more expensive, and you should bear in mind that the more zips you have on a rucksack, the more places there are for water to get in to and the more zips there are to break. Travel packs can be a good option if you are not planning on doing a lot of real trekking or hiking, if you are planning on spending long periods in one place and if you need to arrive somewhere looking smarter than your average backpacker.

When you have found the rucksack that is the right size, the right price and suitable for your journey, do a last check...

☑ Are the seams double or triple sewn? (single is not enough)
☑ Are major seams covered or sealed?
☑ Is the rucksack as waterproof as possible?
☑ Is it made out of heavy-duty nylon?
☑ Is the base of the rucksack thicker than the rest of it?

## What should I pack?

Size may matter but less is definitely more when it comes to packing.

☺ **Tips:**
☑ Pack the heaviest stuff at the bottom and towards the inside of the rucksack (i.e. against your back).
☑ Pack the things which you will need most often near the top. Be ruthless. Books are heavy to carry and you can buy them any where, likewise toiletries.

See the following pages for tips on how to look after yourself and your belongings while you are travelling.

image copyright: Nevada Commission on Tourism

# travel safety

✎ **Note:**

It's worth pointing out the obvious straight away - that since the events of September 11 and the war in Iraq, the US is in a state of high security alert and the authorities, particularly in airports, are not in the mood for messing about. Don't even think about jokingly saying that you've got a bomb in your luggage - it's not funny and it will land you in serious trouble for wasting everybody's time.

That said, the point of this section isn't to scare you. It's just to make sure that you're aware of how to be safe in the many different exciting situations and environments you'll find yourself in.

## Things to watch out for in the cities

☑ Know where your valuables are - always be careful if somebody looks like they're deliberately trying to distract you or invade your personal space. It's probably not them you should be watching, but their friend with the wandering hands!

☑ Walk close to the road so that people can't just jump out at you (but watch cars pulling up along side you too!). In the very rare event that someone does try and mug you, just hand over whatever they want. Nothing you have in your pockets is worth risking life and limb for.

☑ Use your common sense and don't wander around dodgy looking areas, especially after dark - you wouldn't do it at home so don't do it anywhere else.

☑ Be natural and try not to worry too much. If you've never been mugged in Britain, the chances are you must be doing something right, and if you keep on using your common sense, you're more than likely to be OK in the US. If you have been mugged, attacked, hassled or verbally abused before, use that experience to lessen your chances of it happening again.

☑ Just because somewhere is 'abroad' or 'foreign' doesn't necessarily mean it's more dangerous, just as long as you make sure you're aware of local differences in behaviour and attitude.

## Guns

Be aware that there are always risks in a country where it is a citizen's right to 'keep and bear arms'. Never get yourself into a situation where a gun is involved and you put yourself or others at risk. And don't give other people the excuse to use them - whether they're the policeman who's just pulled you over for suspected speeding or a mugger in a dark alley. Be on your guard around guns and always be conscious of the behaviour of the people who own them.

# travel safety

## Things to watch out for in the Great Outdoors

Firstly, always make sure you know...

★ where you're going and make sure that other people know too - they should also know when you're due back.

★ what the weather could be like and that you've got the clothes to deal with it.

★ the potential natural hazards you could meet and how to deal with them if you do.

Please bear in mind that these tips are just guidelines and general advice. As with all new places and experiences, it is essential to get further expert advice and help from professionals on the on the spot. In the meantime, here are some quick tips on potential dangers...

## Poison ivy

If you're into hiking, you're more than likely to encounter poison ivy which can cause nasty skin irritations. It's a low growing plant (make sure you check before you sit down!) that also creeps up trees like British ivy. Each branch has got three dark shiny leaves. If you think you've touched some, try and wash it off with soap and water. If it's in your eyes, see a doctor. Remember 'leaves three, leave it be'.

## Snakes

The rattlesnake is the most common of all North America's poisonous snakes - however, you're unlikely to ever come across one in the wild as they are shy and reclusive, despite their scary reputation. Remember, if you see a snake, stay away from it. Obviously! Snakes are generally not looking for trouble, so make plenty of noise (especially if you find yourself in the wilds at night), and you're unlikely to meet each other unexpectedly. Be careful when you're picking things up - don't stick your hands in places if you can't see what's lurking there!

If you're bitten, as with all snakes, try and see exactly what kind of snake it was that got you - this helps get the medication right. Never put on a tourniquet or try to cut the wound, take off any rings or bracelets you've got on before the wound swells, keep movement to a minimum, put a lightweight bandage around the bite and get to a hospital as quick as you can. Bites from a rattler won't kill you but they are incredibly painful.

# travel safety

## Bears

North America's big bears, the black bear and the grizzly, are generally shy and will try to avoid any contact with humans. The problem comes when some start to try to hassle humans for food, coming close to towns or campsites to see what they can steal. Bears are amazing animals - it's quite something if you do get to see one. Just make sure that you know the 'bear' neccesities to make sure there are no misunderstandings between you and Mr or Mrs Grizzly.

## Remember:

- ☑ Don't travel alone - a big group is noisier and you're less likely to surprise any bears in the area.
- ☑ Avoid areas where you can see scavenging birds circling - it may be the site of a kill and bears won't like you turning up for dinner uninvited.
- ☑ Don't encourage them to come looking for food in your tent - keep all your food away from the camp and hung in trees out of reach, and always clear up your litter.
- ☑ Don't get too close to a bear if you see one - they'll most likely leave you alone if you do the same. Be very careful of mother bears with cubs - she will be very protective of them and is likely to feel more threatened than usual.

## Mountain lions (cougars)

Cougars are very shy creatures that you're really unlikely to meet face-to-face. Pretty much the same general rules apply for cougars as with bears - don't surprise them and try and back out of the situation if you meet one. If it still looks like it wants to eat you, make yourself as big, noisy and human-looking as possible. Honestly.

# travel safety

## Dangers in the desert

The USA has some of the hottest, driest places on earth and there are a few things worth bearing in mind if you're travelling out there...

☑     Beware of rattlesnakes - avoid them if you can, don't annoy them and get medical help as quickly as possible if they bite you.

☑     Always carry enough water for you **and** your car.

☑     Take precautions against heatstroke and sunstroke and, of course, sunburn.

## Tornadoes in the MidWest

Storms can whip up from nowhere in America's flat Mid-West and can devastate whole areas within minutes. Watch the weather, stay alert and bear in mind these general guidelines if you see a twister approaching...

☑     You want to try and get underground if you possibly can - if you haven't got a basement, find someone who has.

☑     If you're out and about, go to the nearest public building and ask if you can join them in the basement.

☑     If you're driving, the best place to be is tucked right under a bridge (get out of your car - tornadoes can easily pick them up and throw them!). And if there's really nothing about that is secure enough to hide under, lie flat on your face as low on the ground as you can.

image copyright: Robert Holmes/CalTour

# travel safety

## Women travellers

You've probably already developed your own personal strategies for dealing with aggressive, unpleasant men, and if they've worked for you in your home country, the chances are they'll work in the US too. However, here are some possible guidelines...

☑ Walk confidently down the street and look as if you know where you're going (even if you don't!)

☑ Try and ignore comments and remarks, but don't ignore dangerous situations as they develop - never allow yourself to become isolated and vulnerable.

☑ Try not to be out and about on your own after dark, and be wary if you're drinking alone. Be careful of what you drink, how much you drink, and make sure nobody puts anything in your drink.

☑ Stay close to other women if possible, whether in the street or on public transport.

☑ Never accept lifts or get into a car if you don't know the driver.

## Gay & lesbian

As a general rule, attitudes towards gay relationships become more conservative the further inland you get in the US. What the locals in San Francisco find acceptable could get you into trouble out in the sticks. Many laws discriminating against gays from state-to-state have recently been declared unconstitutional by the Supreme Court. Despite this, around 20 states still retain some laws on their statutes which outlaw homosexual acts.

## And finally...

Please don't be put off! You could argue that there are lots of ways for you to kill or injure yourself in the USA. However, they are extremely unlikely to happen to you and any fear of them should just encourage you to be prepared and informed. Don't let it put you off getting out there and enjoying yourself.

 www.fco.gov.uk/travel

# travel safety

## Looking after your belongings

There are few things worse than losing your rucksack or belongings when you are away. There will be times when you have to leave your rucksack in vulnerable places, and you'll feel much happier about doing this if you have some security products with which you can protect it. Below are some products we recommend...

- ☑ **Rucksack harness** - protects your rucksack from damage and theft both in transit and when being worn. It is expensive, but think about how much it would cost to replace your rucksack, and everything it contains, if it was lost or stolen.

- ☑ **Waist wallet** - for documents and money. Ideally it should be worn against the skin for total concealment. Try not to have to access a waist wallet when you are in a public place, especially in a bus or train station.

- ☑ **Cable lock** - for securing luggage or skis to an immoveable object.

- ☑ **Padlocks** - ideally with combination rather than key.

- ☑ **Personal attack alarm**.

- ☑ **Door guard** - simple gadget that secures an inward opening door.

- ☑ **Waterproof wallets & cases** - there are many types available, not only for money and documents but also for mobile phones.

- ☑ **First aid kit** - whether you are stuck in a city centre hostel or out in the mountains hiking, it will be useful.

# insurance

Getting the proper insurance is important for your trip. A good gap year policy will be tailored to backpacker's needs. Your luggage as a backpacker is probably only going to consist of a rucksack with a few clothes in it, so most policies don't insure your luggage for a huge amount.

The medical cover you receive is very important when you are away. Even in developed countries like the USA, health services work differently and you may have to pay more for certain things. Medical treatment is very expensive wherever you are, and if something really drastic happened to you whilst you were abroad, the costs could be astronomical. Most gap year insurance packages cover repatriation costs, meaning that they would pay for you to be flown home if you were seriously ill. Some will cover the cost of having a family member flown out to you in an emergency. Knowing you are covered for most eventualities gives you the peace of mind to really enjoy your gap year.

## Navigator

☎    0870 241 0576

✎    www.navigatortravel.co.uk

## Insurance checklist...

☑    How long am I insured for?

☑    Where in the world will the insurance policy cover me?

☑    What happens if I lose or have my passport stolen?

☑    What happens if someone steals my wallet?

☑    Am I covered for extreme sports and adventure activities?

☑    What happens if I need to go hospital?

☑    What happens if I miss my flight?

☑    What happens if I have to do exam retakes?

☑    Will I get flown home if I need to?

# accommodation

## Accommodation

Finding a hostel is made easier at www.hostelworld.com. You can search for hostels all over the world, and even make bookings before you arrive.

Ask yourself the following questions before making a booking:

☑ How much can I spend?
☑ Where do I want to be – central or not?
☑ How long do I need to spend there?
☑ Could I work there?

Many hostels will have facilities for luggage storage, but you may have to resign yourself to the fact that you will have to leave your rucksack unattended in the dormitories at certain times. Just make sure that you carry all your important stuff, documents, money and things of personal value with you. Before you head off travelling make copies of important documents like passports, visas, travellers cheques and save them along with other data on a new site www.travelvault.com which allows you to retrieve them when required anywhere in the world through fax or email.

You can read up details on all the hostels before you head-off at www.hostelworld.com. Hostelworld also feature hostel reviews from other travellers on items such as character, location, fun, security and staff. These are independent reviews from people who have stayed in this hostel before so should give you a good indication of the standard.

If you want to save money on your hostel bookings for a whole year, sign up now for Hostelworld's Gold Membership for just $10 annually and pay no $2 service charges on bookings over a 12 month period

**Some useful accommodation websites:**
 www.hostelworld.com - Book hostels and get info online
 www.hostelusa.com

# getting to the usa

## Flights

Getting a flight to the USA is pretty straightforward. It's one of the top flight destinations from the UK and Ireland, Australia and New Zealand, and isn't exactly short on international airports. The internet is always a good place to start looking for cheap flights, but there are plenty of more traditional ways too. Pop into your local travel agent, keep an eye out for ads in the paper and don't forget to take a look at trusty old Ceefax or Teletext (it's really very good!).

Prices vary depending on when you go and obviously where you go. Around November to March is the low season (with the notable and very expensive exception of the Christmas season and the winter resorts), and prices are a bit cheaper then than for the rest of the year. Whatever the time of year, there are usually bargains to be had.

The main international airports are listed below but you'll probably have to change if you want to fly to a smaller city.

Honolulu - San Francisco - Washington DC - Boston - Miami - Dallas - Fort Worth - Seattle - Houston - Chicago - New York - Newark - Atlanta - LA

As a rough guide, flights from the UK to the East Coast take around 7 or 8 hours, and 12 to 13 hours to the West Coast.

## Airlines to the USA from the UK & Ireland

- American Airlines - www.americanairlines.com
- British Airways - www.ba.com
- Cathay Pacific - www.cathaypacific.com
- Delta Airlines - www.delta-air.com
- KLM - www.klm.com
- Pan Am World Airways - www.carnivalair.com
- Qantas - www.qantas.com
- TWA Transworld Airlines - www.twa.com
- United Airlines - www.ual.com
- US Airways - www.usairways.com
- World Airways - www.worldair.com

# getting to the usa

## ...& from Australia & New Zealand to the USA

- Air New Zealand - www.airnz.co.nz
- Singapore Airlines - www.singaporeair.com
- Qantas - www.qantas.com.au
- United Airlines - www.ual.com
- Air Pacific - www.airpacific.galileo.com
- Cathay Pacific - www.cathaypacific.com

## Jet lag

One of the main problems with long haul flights is that crossing time zones disrupts your sleep patterns and causes jet lag. Travelling eastwards is more likely to make you jetlagged than going west. Symptoms include tiredness, irritability, forgetfulness and disorientation. This can be a real problem if you have to cope with feeling jet lagged as well as arriving in a strange country. You can help prevent jet lag by getting a good night's sleep the night before you travel, drinking plenty of water, stretching regularly during the flight and taking daytime flights.

To give yourself time to adapt to new time zones and recover from jet lag, allow one day's recovery for every time zone you cross.

## Economy class syndrome

Travelling for hours on a plane is not good for your circulation. Economy Class Syndrome is the commonly used name for deep vein thrombosis (DVT). DVT happens when a blood clot forms after being sat in cramped conditions for a long period of time. It is relatively rare, but research on the subject shows that it may be more of a problem than previously thought. The condition can be fatal.

By simply moving around during the flight, walking up and down the aisle, stretching and drinking plenty of water you reduce the chances of contracting DVT. Taking sleeping pills or drinking excessive alcohol during the flight is not recommended. The more mobile and active you are, the better. Smokers, obese people and women who are pregnant or using the contraceptive pill are at more risk of developing DVT.

# getting around

It's nearly 2,800 miles from New York to San Diego - that's over twice the distance from London to Kiev. The United States are massive and, if you want to see lots of cities, you're going to have to plan well and allow lots of time. If time is limited, it's much better to visit fewer places for longer. Be realistic and think about your itinerary - how much time you have, where you can get work, when you have to be there, how much money you've got and, of course, where you want to go!

With most people's 'local' foodstore a good two hours drive away from their home (OK, we're exaggerating a little bit), it's no surprise that it's often much quicker to fly between many US cities. We've also included some useful info on getting around by road and rail.

## By air

The major domestic airlines in the US cover pretty much most of the major cities, but it's also worth keeping an eye open for good deals with some of the budget airlines listed below. Bear in mind that flights are generally cheaper in the middle of the week:

★    **Song** fly between Los Angeles, Las Vegas, Boston, Hartford, New York, Washington, Atlanta, Orlando, Tampa, Fort Lauderdale, West Palm Beach, Fort Myers and San Juan, the capital of Puerto Rico.

⬟    www.flysong.com

★    **JetBlue** fly between Seattle, Oakland, Long Beach, San Diego, Salt Lake City, Denver, Vegas, Atlanta, New Orleans, Buffalo, Rochester, Syracuse, Burlington, New York, Washington DC, Orlando, Tampa, West Palm Beach and Fort Lauderdale.

⬟    www.jetblue.com

Other low fare carriers include Southwest, AirTran, Frontier and American Trans Air.

⬟    www.iflyswa.com

⬟    www.airtran.com

⬟    www.frontierairlines.com

⬟    www.ata.com

# getting around

## By road

Bus travel is a good way of reaching those places that train and planes can't get to. The bus network is pretty comprehensive and easy to use. Greyhound Buses go all over the USA - over 20,000 daily departures to more than 3,700 locations in 48 states - and offer good value for money with their passes, particularly if you book in advance.

A North America Discovery Pass gives you unlimited travel from between 4 and 60 days. You can take advantage of a 25% discount for students if you have an ISIC card or 10% discount if you have a VIP or Nomad's card.

     www.greyhound.com

## Backpacker tours

If you want a great travel experience with like-minded people and catch those major sites and attractions on the way, Contiki Holidays for 18-35s offer unique tours. You can travel by air conditioned coach on loads of trips including the Alaskan Explorer, Hawaiian Discovery, LA to the Bay and California Highlights. Accommodation and meals are included in the tours.

     www.contiki.com

Green Tortoise works on the basis that 'beautiful places, good food and sociable people with an enthusiasm for life and nature, are the only essentials for economical and gratifying travel experiences'. Not a bad philosophy if you are wanting to see the US by coach. Trips include Yosemite National Park, Coast to Coast, Death Valley National Park, Canyons of the West, an Alaskan expedition and Cross Country Eastbound. A three day tour of the Yosemite National Park costs $134 (plus $46 food fund) while a 12 day Eastbound trip costs $499 (plus $131 for the food fund). Check out their website for up-to-date trips and fares...

     www.greentortoise.com

# getting around

## Driving

As a visitor, you can drive in the United States if you have a UK valid drivers license (but not a provisional one). If you are entering as a temporary resident you need to get a driving license from the appropriate state authority when you arrive.

Driving laws vary from state to state. Speed limits are measured in miles per hour like the UK but make sure you check the road signs, as speed limits can vary a lot. As a general rule you could follow this...

Motorways - 75mph
Urban stretches - 70mph
Dual carriageways - 65mph
Outside built-up areas - 50-65mph
Built-up areas - 25-35mph

Speed limits are strictly enforced in many states, especially the highly populated eastern areas. In the western states, enforcement can be much more lax and motorists often drive at 85mph or more. For more information and advice, check out...

     www.drivingabroad.co.uk


✎     **Note:**
Speed and drink driving limits are lower than in the UK.

If you are planning to hire a car in the United States you are advised to get an International Driving Permit before you leave the UK. Most car hire firms insist that you need to have held a full license for at least one year. The minimum age for hiring a car is 21, although it can be as high as 25, and there is often an additional charge for drivers who are under 25. Here are just some of the many national car hire companies in the US...

     www.alamo.com
     www.avis.com
     www.dollar.com
     www.hertz.com
     www.thrifty.com

## By rail

Amtrak links 500 communities in 46 states (not including Alaska, Hawaii, South Dakota and Wyoming). You can get up to date travel information and make reservations directly at their website...

 www.amtrak.com

And here's some highly recommended routes...

★ **The Coast Starlight** - one of Amtrak's most scenic trips and a particular favourite with gappers. There's often a bit of a party atmosphere, starting in the lounge car and spreading through the train as it travels between Seattle and Los Angeles. You see snow-covered mountains, forest valleys and long stretches of the Pacific shoreline. Dreamy!

★ **The California Zephyr** - Takes two days and nights to travel between Chicago and San Francisco, crossing farmland, prairie, deserts, rivers and the Rocky Mountains. A mere 2,420 mile journey.

★ **The Southwest Chief -** Amtrak's fastest trip from Chicago to the Pacific - 2,230 miles through eight states, passing wheat fields, ranches, missions, pueblos, mountains and deserts.

★ **The Sunset Limited -** The only way to travel from coast to coast on a single train. After going north from Orlando to Jacksonville in Florida the train heads west.

 www.usa-by-rail.com

# communications

## Telephones

## Making calls internationally

☎   To call the US from the UK, dial 001 + city/area code + local number

☎   To call the UK from the US dial 01 + 44 + city/area code (minus 0) + local number

☎   To call Australia from the US dial 01 + 61 + city/area code + local number

☎   To call New Zealand from the US dial 01 + 64 + city/area code + local number

It's cheaper to call overseas off peak. Off peak times vary, depending on where you want to phone. If you are using public payphones, which can be found on most streets and public places, use either 25 cents for a three minute local call, or a phonecard. You can buy phonecards in newsagents and shops that offer cheap international calls.

## Regional dialling codes

In the US, you have to dial a '1' first if you are calling a number outside your area code.

☎   Austin - 512
☎   Atlanta - 404
☎   Boston - 617
☎   Chicago - 312
☎   Denver - 303
☎   Honolulu - 808
☎   Houston - 713
☎   Las Vegas - 702
☎   Los Angeles - 213
☎   Miami - 305
☎   New Orleans - 504
☎   New York (Bronx, Brooklyn, Queens, Staten Island) - 718
☎   New York (Manhattan) - 212
☎   Philadelphia - 215
☎   Phoenix - 602
☎   Portland - 503

☎     Raleigh - 919
☎     St Louis - 314
☎     San Diego - 619
☎     San Francisco - 415
☎     Seattle - 206
☎     Washington DC - 202

## Useful numbers

☎     Operator - dial 0
☎     Emergency - 911

## Toll free numbers

'Toll free' numbers are freecall numbers. You'll find that many hostels, hotels, resorts and businesses use them. You can recognise them easily because they begin with 800, 888 or 877. But be aware that if a number begins 900 it means it's a premium rate line and, more often than not, a chatline.

## Mobile phones

Mobile phones are popular in the US, and if you are planning on applying for a lot of jobs they can be useful, as it means employers can keep in touch with you. You can either buy a handset with a 'pay as you go' option or subscribe to a contracted price plan.

## Time zones

★     Hawaii is 10 hours behind GMT (Honolulu).
★     Alaska is 9 hours behind GMT (Anchorage).
★     USA Pacific is 8 hours behind GMT (Portland, San Francisco, San Diego).
★     USA Mountain is 7 hours behind GMT (Denver, Salt Lake City).
★     USA Central is 6 hours behind GMT (Dallas, Chicago, St Louis, NewOrleans).
★     USA Eastern is 5 hours behind GMT (New York, Miami, Washington DC, Boston).

# glossary

In a nation as ethnically diverse as the USA, it's no surprise that there is no single official language for the country (though there is for some states). The majority of people in the States speak American English and/or Spanish, but there are literally hundreds of other languages spoken by people as their first language at home. Being the helpful people we are, we've provided a collection of useful phrases in Spanish, as well as clearing up a few areas of confusion between American and British English - there is a difference!

## Some basic Spanish phrases

| | |
|---|---|
| Yes | Sí |
| No | No |
| Please | Por favor |
| Thank you | Gracias |
| Sorry | Disculpe |
| You're welcome | De nada |
| Hello | Hola |
| Good morning | Buenos días |
| Goodbye | Adiós |
| Good evening | Buenas noches |
| See you later | Hasta luego |
| Please speak more slowly | Hable más despacio, por favor |
| I'm sorry, I don't speak Spanish | Lo siento, no hablo español |
| Do you speak English? | Habla usted inglés? |

## American & British English

The English that our friends in the US speak is not the same as British English, and it's worth remembering a few of the differences to prevent confusion, and in some cases embarrassment...

| We say.... | They say... |
|---|---|
| aubergine | eggplant |
| autumn | fall |
| bum bag | fanny pack |
| café | diner |
| current account | checking account |
| engaged (on phone) | busy signal |
| indicator (on car) | turn signal |
| petrol | gasoline/gas |
| roundabout | traffic circle |
| tap (for water) | faucet |
| tights | pantyhose |
| pavement | sidewalk |
| sweets | candy |

## Banks

The US dollar is divided into 100 cents.
Australian $1 = 0.64 US $
British £1 = 1.57 US $
Euro 1 = 1.08 US $
New Zealand $1 = 0.56 US $ *

 www.oanda.com

There are a handful of main banks in the US that have branches across the country. While opening a bank account isn't difficult, it is best to shop around for one. Banks in the US seem to charge for everything, including ATM (cashpoint) withdrawals, so try to ensure that you open an account that either has so many free withdrawals per month or has lower fees.

 www.bankofamerica.com - Bank of America
 www.bankone.com - Bank One
 www.chase.com - Chase
 www.citibank.com - Citibank
www.usbank.com - US Bank

## Tax

Almost everything you pay for in the USA is taxed. Be warned that the tax on meals and drinks, accommodation and most things you buy is added to the price. Occasionally tax is included in the price, like drinks at a bar. A few states have no sales tax and in others it varies up to about 8%. There may also be local and city sales taxes (between 5% and 8%).

Find out more about sales tax and paying tax from the US Inland Revenue at...

 www.irs.gov

It makes for fascinating reading, but basically bear in mind that your pay will have a chunk taken out of it by the US government. If you want to find out about claiming tax back from overseas earnings, go to...

 www.taxback.com

*Correct at time of going to press

## Healthcare

The public healthcare system is practically non-existent in the United States and private healthcare costs a lot. If you're planning on skiing, snowboarding, white water rafting or anything else that runs the risk of bodily injury - get insured (see out insurance section on page 41). Take out a policy that covers you for all eventualities, including immediate expenses (you have to pay for medicine and care upfront) and emergency repatriation. Most of the destinations in this book list hospitals under the 'Emergencies' section.

There are no vaccination requirements for travellers entering the US.

## Embassies

An embassy or consulate is in charge of looking after their citizens' interests in foreign countries. Washington DC, as the capital of the USA, is home to the embassies of Australia, New Zealand, Great Britain and Ireland. If you run into serious trouble while you are away, contact your embassy or consular representative. As a preventative measure, you could check out the British Foreign and Commonwealth Office website at...

    www.fco.gov.uk

### Australian Embassy
✉    1601 Massachusetts Avenue, Washington DC 20036
☎    202 797 3000

### British Embassy
✉    3100 Massachusetts Avenue, Washington DC 20008
☎    202 588 7800

### Irish Embassy
✉    2234 Massachusetts Avenue, Washington DC 20008
☎    202 462 3939

### New Zealand Embassy
✉    37 Observatory Circle, Washington DC 20008
☎    202 328 4800

# destinations introduction

In the next section of the book we cover potential work opportunities on a city by city basis. The section is divided into the areas that are the best source of temporary work.

After some touristy information about each destination, including top things to do and places to stay, there are listings of hotels, bars, employment agencies and other sources of work specific to the city. Once you have this information it is entirely up to you how you use it. You could contact the hotels or bars from home and find out if they will need any staff when you arrive there. You could call the employment agencies to find out if they would be interested in your skills, or contact major employers to set up a work placement.

## At a glance...

### North East Coast
Boston - New York - Philidelphia - Washington DC

### South & Florida
Atlanta - Austin - Houston - Miami - New Orleans - Raleigh

### North West Coast & California
Los Angeles - Portland - San Diego - San Francisco - Seattle -

### South West
Las Vegas - Phoenix

### Rocky Mountains, Great Plains & Great Lakes
Chicago - Denver - St Louis

### Hawaii
Honolulu

The states of New York, New Jersey, Maine, New Hampshire, Massachusetts, Vermont, Connecticut, Pennsylvania, Delaware and Maryland are among the oldest and most beautiful states in the USA. There's an incredible diversity of things to do and see, from the staggering buzz of New York City to the roar of Niagara Falls, from the glitz of Manhattan to the old world rural charm of the New England states. We're concentrating on the cities and resorts, because that's where your best chance of getting work is, but the USA isn't just about glittering skyscrapers - it's also got some of the most spectacular natural wonders in the world. Make sure you take time to check them out.

image courtesy of Massachusetts Office of Travel & Tourism

## Why Boston?

New England is a green, quaint and leafy corner of the USA, and Boston is at its old-fashioned heart. Boston has always had a reputation for free thinking and rebellion. It was one of the places where the American Revolution was born. But it's now also a city that has struck a startling balance between old and new. You'll find skyscrapers and old colonial buildings, horrendous roads but a great underground system, all coming together to make an entertaining place to live. With a distinguished academic tradition (Harvard is just over the river) Boston feels the influence of its great universities and great thinkers through its architecture and history, its modern vibrancy and its old world charm.

## Some Boston facts...

★ Boston has the world's smallest suspension bridge.

★ Harvard University is actually in a city called Cambridge, over the Charles River from Boston.

## Top things to do in Boston...

★ Wander around the Freedom Trail - a fascinating behind-the-scenes look at the drama of the American Revolution, and the Black Heritage Trail - Boston's 19th century black community on Beacon Hill.

★ Do a wee spot of whale watching on a harbour trip.

★ Have a swift beer at the Cheers Beacon Hill, the restaurant and bar that inspired the television show 'Cheers' (where everybody knows your name...).

★ Get cultural - choose from the Boston Symphony Orchestra, the Boston Ballet, national and local theatre productions or the art museums (the Museum of Fine Arts, the Isabella Stewart Gardner Museum and the Institute of Contemporary Art to name just a few).

★ Take a slow ride on the public garden's famous swan boats. Very relaxing.

★ If you're feeling particularly worthy, absorb yourself in American history at the Kennedy Library and Museum.

### Greater Boston Convention & Visitors Bureau

Two Copley Place, Suite 105

www.bostonusa.com

# boston

## Getting there

Boston's Logan Airport tends to get very busy. It serves the whole state of Massachusetts and has good links.

The subway runs from the airport straight into Boston. The 'blue line' is quick but tends to get quite crowded during the rush hour. If you have a lot of baggage consider taking the commuter rail. It's more comfortable but a little bit slower. You can also travel by boat from the airport to Boston downtown - a one way ticket is around $5.

There are three main railway stations in Boston. Back Bay and North Station are both run by Amtrak. South Station is a smaller station and tends to be used more by local trains. If you are arriving by bus, the Greyhound bus terminal is on Atlantic Avenue by the South Station.

## Getting around

Massachusetts Bay Transportation Authority (MBTA) runs Boston's public transport. For a quick journey to the other side of the city, use the subway - a single ticket only costs $1. But if you can't get to where you want to by subway then try the buses. They are cheap and usually run on-time. And you can get a 10-ride ticket or weekly pass.

For more information about the fares and routes on MBTA...

 617 222 5218

 www.mbta.com

## Accommodation

### Hostels

★ **Abercrombie Farrington Inn**, 23 Farrington Avenue - 617 787 1860

★ **Beantown Hostel**, 222-224 Friend Street - 617 723 0800

★ **Boston's Irish Embassy Hostel**, 232 Friend Street - 617 973 4841

★ **HI-Boston Back Bay Summer Ayh Hostel**, 519 Beacon Street - 617 353 3294

★ **HI-Boston at Fenway**, 575 Commonwealth Avenue - 617 267 8599

★ **HI-Boston International Hostel**, 12 Hemenway Street - 617 536 9455

★ **The Prescott International Hotel & Hostel**, 36 Church Street, Everett - 617 389 1990

### Camping

★ **Boston National Historic Park**, Charlestown Navy Yard - 617 242 5642, www.nps.gov

★ **Beach Rose RV Park**, 147 Beach Road Salisbury - 978 463 0226

image copyright: Massachusetts Office of Travel & Tourism

north east coast

# boston

## Work

Boston's mix of the traditional and the modern gives it a great mix of opportunities for people looking for work. From waiting to IT temping for some of America's (and the world's) biggest companies, the jobs are there.

## Bar work

★     **An Tain**, 31 India Street - 617 426 1870
★     **An Tua Nua**, 835 Beacon Street - 617 262 2121
★     **The Black Rose**, 160 State Street - 617 742 2281
★     **Clerys**, 113 Dartmouth Street - 617 262 9874
★     **Coogan's Bluff**, 173 Milk Street - 617 451 7415
★     **The Dubliner**, 14/16 Bromfield Street - 617 357 1899
★     **Grafton Street**, 1274 Massachusetts Avenue - 617 867 9090
★     **The Grand Canal**, 57 Canal Street - 617 523 1112
★     **Green Dragon Tavern**, 11 Marshall Street - 617 367 0055
★     **Hibernia**, 25 Kingston Street - 617 292 2333
★     **Hurricane O'Reilly's**, 150 Canal Street - 617 722 0161
★     **The Irish Embassy Pub**, 234 Friend Street - 617 742 6618
★     **JJ Foley's**, 21 Kingston Street - 617 338 7713
★     **Jose McIntyre's**, 160 Milk Street - 617 451 9460
★     **Kennedy's Midtown**, 42 Province Street - 888 832 6350
★     **The Kinsale**, 2 Centre Plaza - 617 742 5577
★     **The Last Hurrah**, 60 School Street - 617 227 8600
★     **The Littlest Bar**, 47 Province Street - 617 523 9766
★     **McCarthy's Restaurant**, 903 Boylston Street - 617 867 9090
★     **McGann's**, 197 Portland Street - 617 227 4059
★     **Michael Sherlock's Pub & Restaurant**, 99 Broad Street - 617 350 7077
★     **MJ O'Connor's**, 27 Columbus Avenue - 617 482 2255
★     **Molly Darcy's Pub & Restaurant**, 658 E Broadway - 617 268 1177
★     **Mr Dooley's Boston Tavern**, 77 Broad Street - 617 338 5656
★     **Paddy Burke's**, 132 Portland Street - 617 367 8370
★     **Pat Flannigan's**, 804 Huntington Avenue - 617 730 5522
★     **The Purple Shamrock**, 1 Union Street - 617 227 2060
★     **The Times Pub & Restaurant**, 112 Broad Street - 617 357 8463

## Hotel work

★ **Boston Backbay Hilton Hotel**, 40 Dalton Street - 617 867 6000

★ **Hilton's**, 272 Friend Street - 617 227 9104

★ **Hotel Sheraton Boston**, Prudential Center - 617 236 2000

★ **Hyatt Harborside**, 101 Harborside Drive - 617 568 1234

★ **ITT Sheraton Corporation** - 617 367 3600

★ **Nine Zero Hotel**, 90 Tremont Street - 617 772 5800

★ **Park Plaza Hotel & Towers in Boston**, 64 Arlington Street - 617 426 2000

★ **Radisson Hotel Boston**, 200 Stuart Street - 617 482 1800

★ **Ramada Inn Boston**, 800 William T Morrissey - 617 287 9101

★ **Regal Bostonian Hotel**, 26 North Street - 617 523 3600

★ **Ritz Carlton Boston**, 15 Arlington Street - 617 536 5700

★ **Ritz Carlton Boston Commons**, 2 Avery Street - 617 574 7100

★ **Sheraton Boston Hotel & Towers**, 39 Dalton Street - 617 236 2000

## Language school work

★ **Boston Academy of English**, 395 Washington Street - 617 338 6243

★ **Boston Language Institute**, 636 Beacon Street - 617 262 3500

★ **English Language Centre**, 867 Boylston Street - 617 536 9788

★ **Learn English**, 1200 Washington Street - 617 426 4319

★ **Thoreau Language Institute,** 63 Melcher Street - 617 426 2600

# boston

## Office work

- ★ **A Best Temp**, 301 W Broadway - 617 269 8885
- ★ **Account Source**, 133 Federal Street - 617 556 0100
- ★ **Adecco**, Boston Place - 617 523 5030
- ★ **Bay State Temp**, 1444 Dorchester Avenue - 617 825 8721
- ★ **Bradford Group Tempories**, 100 Franklin Street - 617 338 9922
- ★ **Brattle Temps**, 50 Congress Street - 617 523 4600
- ★ **Bulfinch Temporary Service**, 101 Merrimac Street - 617 726 5858
- ★ **Eagle Temp Service**, 243 Bowdoin Street - 617 436 3740
- ★ **Four Season Temporary**, 13 Clover Street - 617 282 8414
- ★ **Manpower**, 4 Train Street - 617 288 2324
- ★ **Marathon Temps**, 33 Broad Street - 617 557 9988
- ★ **Millennium 2000 Temp**, 1444 Dorchester Avenue - 617 825 9700
- ★ **Office Power**, 99 Chaucy Street - 617 482 0586
- ★ **Preferred Temporaries**, 100 City Hall Plaza - 617 723 1919
- ★ **Scott-Wayne Temporaries**, 100 Charles River Plaza - 617 720 9000
- ★ **Systemp**, 31 Saint James Avenue - 617 542 1700
- ★ **Temp Center**, 383 Dorchester Avenue - 617 268 4234
- ★ **Temporary Help Affiliates**, 129 Tremont Street - 617 423 2986
- ★ **Word Perfect Temporaries**, 3 Center Plaza - 617 367 6665

## IT agencies

- ★ **Aardvark Systems & Programming**, 129 South Street - 617 423 8830
- ★ **PC Help Services**, 10 High Street - 617 482 2201
- ★ **Sapphire Technologies**, 50 Milk Street - 617 357 4668
- ★ **Spherion Technology**, 800 Boylston Street - 617 542 1700
- ★ **Techsource**, 204 Adams Street - 617 825 2009

## Communications

### Internet cafés
★    **Adrenaline Zone**, 40 Battle Street - 617 876 1314
★    **Designs for Living**, 52 Queensberry Street - 617 536 6150

### Library
★    **The Boston Central Public Library,** 700 Boylston Street - 617 536 5400, info@bpl.org

## Emergencies

**Police**
▤    City of Boston Police Department, 7 Warren Avenue
☎    617 343 4250

**British Consulate-General Boston**
▤    One Memorial Drive, Suite 1500, Cambridge
☎    617 245 4500
🏯    www.britainusa.com/consular/boston

**Massachusetts General Hospital**
▤    55 Fruit Street
☎    617 726 2787

north east coast

image copyright: Massachusetts Office of Travel & Tourism

# new york

## Why New York?

If you have to ask, you've obviously never watched an American film or seen an American cop series, never listened to hip hop or to Bob Dylan, or wondered where pretty much all of the world's most famous paintings have ended up. The city oozes excitement and almost every turn brings up fresh images of the fantasy America that the rest of the world knows through film and TV. The city itself is the star and the opportunities for sight-seeing, entertainment and spending your hard-earned cash are pretty much limitless. See how many New York film clichés you can spot, from steaming man-hole covers to fat cops eating doughnuts - it's all there!

## Some New York facts
★  New York City has the largest population of any city in the USA
★  New York State has more places to go skiing than any other state in the US
★  The Statue of Liberty is in the state of New Jersey, not New York.
★  It was given to the people of the USA by the French.
★  And it's got an eight feet long index finger!

## Top things to do in New York...
★  Walk across the Brooklyn Bridge for great views of the Manhattan skyline.
★  If you've a head for heights, why not be one of the 22,000 people to take the daily trek up the Empire State Building - the 86th floor observatory is open air and only 1,050 feet up!
★  Go walking, running, cycling or skating in Central Park and, while you're there, take a peek at the Bethesda Fountain and Conservatory Garden.
★  A stay in New York isn't complete without a cappuccino in Greenwich Village ('the Village') while watching the street musicians, skateboarders, jugglers, stand-up comics and chess players.
★  If food is your thing, then Chinatown is your place - there's restaurants, markets, foods shops and more. So if it's Hunan, Szechuan, Cantonese, Mandarin or Shanghai culinary delights that you're after...
★  The Museum of Modern Art (MoMA) might be off limits for a couple more years with its $650 million reconstruction but that doesn't mean that you have to miss out. Check out its temporary close cousin, MoMA Queens, in Long Island City, Queens for both permanent and changing exhibitions.

★ For ten days every September you can celebrate the Feast of San Gennaro in Little Italy when Mulberry Street becomes one big open air restaurant.

★ Take in a game with the New York Yankees - baseball doesn't get any more real than this.

★ For modern art lovers, the Guggenheim Museum is a must. It boasts Vasily Kandinsky, Paul Klee, Pablo Picasso, Toulouse-Lautrec and Cezanne.

★ Absorb the enormity of the September 11 tragedy by visiting Ground Zero.

## NYC Convention & Visitors Bureau

810 Seventh Avenue
212 484 1271
www.nycvisit.com

image copyright: BUNAC

# new york

## Getting there

There are two main international airports serving New York - John F Kennedy and Newark in New Jersey. If you are arriving at JFK, the best and the quickest way to the city centre is to take a bus to Howard Beach subway station and then take the A line to Manhattan.

There are also airport buses that run between the airport and the city. The New York airport express service bus is reliable and quite fast and it goes straight to Manhattan. A one way ticket costs $13. The Q3 bus also goes to the city centre - it's not as fast but the fare is only $2.

If you are arriving at Newark Airport, it's best to take the airport buses to the city centre. Again, the New York airport express service bus is the quickest and the easiest and goes straight to Manhattan. The fare is around $12.

## By rail

If you are coming to New York on an Amtrak train, you will arrive at Pennsylvania Station. The station is used by Amtrak, Long Island Railroad, New Jersey Transit and Port Authority Trans Hudson and is underneath the Penn Plaza Office Building and Madison Square Garden.

### ✎ Note:
If you are ever leaving by train from Grand Central Station, don't get freaked out by the masses of people you come across. Grand Central Station is the main railway station in New York and it's one of the busiest stations in the world.

## By bus

The Port Authority is the main bus terminal in New York and has services all over the country. George Washington Bridge bus station, the second largest, is uptown with services to New Jersey and Rockland County.

## Getting around

The best and quickest way to get around New York is by subway. A one day pass costs only $4 and you can use it on the buses as well. There's also the seven day unlimited ride card for $17.

For more information about the fares and subway maps visit the Metropolitan Transportation Authority website.

 www.mta.nyc.ny.us

And you can always get around by yellow cabs but it does get expensive if you are stuck in traffic!

## Accommodation

### Hostels

★ **American Dream Hostel**, 168 East 24th Street - 212 260 9779

★ **Big Apple Hostel**, 119 West 45th Street - 212 302 2603, info@bigapplehostel.com, www.bigapplehostel.com

★ **Bowery's Whitehouse Hotel**, 340 Bowery - 212 477 5623, www.whitehousehotelofny.com/index.html

★ **Central Park Hostel**, 19 West 103rd Street near Central Park West - 212 678 0491, info@centralparkhostel.com, www.centralparkhostel.com

★ **Chelsea Center**, 313 West 29th Street - 212 643 0214, info@chelseacenterhostel.com, www.chelseacenterhostel.com

★ **Chelsea International Hostel**, 251 West 20th Street - 212 647 0010

★ **Chelsea Star Hotel**, 300 West 30th Street - 212 244 7827, reservations@starhotelny.com, www.chelseastar.com

★ **The Gershwin Hotel**, 7 East 27th Street - 212 545 8000, reservations@gershwinhostel.com, www.gershwinhostel.com

★ **Guesthouse**, 63 Audubon Avenue - 212 781 1842, germanf@webtv.net, http://community.webtv.net/germanf/doc

★ **Hostelling International New York**, 891 Amsterdam Avenue - 212 932 2300, www.hinewyork.org

★ **Hostel Columbus Circle**, Broadway & 55th Street - 212 397 9686

★ **International Student Center**, 38 West 88th Street - 212 787 7706, info@nystudentcenter.org, www.nystudentcenter.org

# new york

- ★ **Jazz on the Park**, 36 West 106th Street - 212 932 1600
- ★ **Manhattan Youth Castle**, 1596 Lexington Avenue @ 101 - 212 831 4440
- ★ **New York Bed and Breakfast**, 134 West 119th Street - 212 666 0559, newyorkbandb@aol.com
- ★ **New York Connection**, 197 Humbolt Street, Brooklyn - 718 386 5539
- ★ **Sugar Hill International House**, 722 Saint Nicholas Avenue - 212 926 7030, info@sugarhillhostel.com, www.sugarhillhostel.com
- ★ **Uptown Hostel**, 239 Lenox Avenue - 212 666 0559

## Camping (New York State)

- ★ **Battenkill Riversport & Campground**, 937 State RT, 313 Cambridge - 518 677 8868
- ★ **Eastern Long Island Campground**, RT 48 Queen Street, Greenport - 631 477 0022, mydon1@aol.com
- ★ **Niagara Falls**, 2570 Grand Island Boulevard, Grand Island - 712 773 7583
- ★ **Rodout Valley**, PO Box 100, 105 Mettacahonts Road, Accord - 845 625 5521,rvsdr@aol.com
- ★ **SoHi Campground**, 425 Woodland Road, Accord - 845 678 7377, www.sohicampground.com
- ★ **Wigway Keuka Lake Campground**, 3324 Esperanza Road, Bluff Point - 315 536 6352

⬠ www.gocampingamerica.com

## Work

As you would expect in one of the world's most happening cities, there's plenty of bar, hotel and even theatre work available in the Big Apple. You could find yourself in a 70th floor office in a skyscraper in Manhattan, or showing people to their seats in a New York cinema. Enjoy!

## Bar work

★   **Abbey Tavern**, 354 Third Avenue (at 26th Street) - 212 532 1978

★   **Baker Street Pub**, 1152 First Avenue (at 63rd Street) - 212 688 9663

★   **Blarney Star**, 43 Murray Street - 212 732 2873, www.blarneystar.com

★   **Brew's**, 156 E 34th Street (between Lexington & 3rd Avenue) - 212 889 3369, brewsbar@erols.com, www.brewsnyc.com

★   **British Open**, 320 E 59th Street - 212 355 8467, www.britishopen.citysearch.com

★   **Connolly's Pub**, 14 E 47th Street - 212 867 3767

★   **Deacon Brodies**, 370 W 46th Street (between 8th & 9th Avenue) - 212 262 1452

★   **Doc Watson's**, 1490 Second Avenue (between 77th & 78th Streets) - 212 988 5300, info@docwatsons.com, www.docwatsons.com

★   **Dublin House**, 225 W 79th Street - 212 874 9528

★   **Eamonn Doran's**, 998 Second Avenue (between 52nd & 53rd Streets) - 212 753 9191

★   **Emerald Saloon**, 618 Amsterdam Avenue (90th Street) - 212 787 9628

★   **Finnegan's Wake**, 1361 First Avenue (at 73rd Street) - 212 737 3664

★   **Fiona's Bar & Restaurant**, 1664 First Avenue - 212 348 3783

★   **Flannery's Bar**, 205 W 14th Street - 212 229 2122

★   **Gaf Bar**, 254 E 85th Street - 212 472 8176

★   **Glocca Morra Pub**, 304 Third Avenue (at 23rd Street) - 212 473 9638

★   **h2k**, 219 Ninth Avenue (crosses 23rd Street) - 212 727 2616

★   **Hooligan's Tavern**, 1804 Second Avenue (between 93rd & 94th Streets) - 212 289 2273, www.bigdoc.com/hooligans

**north east coast**

**north east coast**

- ★ **Iggy's**, 132 Ludlow Street (at Rivington Street) - 212 529 2731
- ★ **Irish Times**, 1803 Second Avenue (at E 93rd Street) - 212 426 8100
- ★ **Jim Brady's**, 75 Maiden Lane - 212 425 1300
- ★ **Joe's Pub,** 425 LaFayette - 212 539 8778, www.joespub.com
- ★ **Kinsale Tavern**, 1672 Third Avenue (between 93rd & 94th Streets) - 212 348 4370
- ★ **Local 138,** 138 Ludlow Street - 212 477 0280
- ★ **Marty O'Brien's**, 1696 Second Avenue (between 87th & 88th Street) - 212 722 3889
- ★ **McGee's,** 240 W 55th Street(between Broadway & 8th Avenue), - 212 957 3536
- ★ **Molly's**, 287 Third Avenue - 212 889 3361
- ★ **Mustang Harry's**, 352 Seventh Avenue (between 29th & 30th Streets) - 212 268 8930
- ★ **Nevada Smiths**, 74 Third Avenue (between 11th & 12th Streets) - 212 982 2591
- ★ **North Star Pub**, 93 South Street - 212 509 6757, www.northstarpub.com
- ★ **O'Neal's Grand Street**, 174 Grand Street (between Center & Mulberry) - 212 941 9119
- ★ **Old Town Bar & Restaurant**, 45 E 18th Street - 212 529 6732
- ★ **The Parlour**, 250 W 86th Street (between Broadway & West End) - 212 580 8923
- ★ **PJ Carney's**, 906 Seventh Avenue - 212 753 6440, desmondny@yahoo.com, www.pjcarneys.com
- ★ **Peculier Pub**, 145 Bleecker Street - 212 353 1327
- ★ **Playwright Tavern & Restaurant**, 202 W 49th Street - 212 262 9263
- ★ **Rivertown Lounge**, 187 Orchard Street (between Houston & Stanton Streets) - 212 388 1288
- ★ **Scruffy Duffy's**, 743 Eighth Avenue - 212 245 9126
- ★ **Swift's Hibernian Lounge**, 34 E 40th Street (between Lafeyette & Bowery) - 212 260 3600
- ★ **Tir Na Nog Bar & Grill**, 5 Pennsylvania Plaza (between 33rd & 34th Streets) - 212 630 0249
- ★ **Wicked Wolf**, 1142 First Avenue - 212 861 4670

## Hotel work

★ **Four Seasons Hotel New York**, 57 E 57th Street - 212 758 5700
★ **Four Seasons Nevis Sales**, 505 Park Avenue - 212 935 4955
★ **Hilton**, 301 Park Avenue - 212 872 1324
★ **Hilton**, 230 W 41st Street - 212 840 8222
★ **Hilton**, 3 E 54th Street - 212 751 9022
★ **Mark Hotel**, 25 E 77th Street - 212 744 4300
★ **Marriott Hotels & Resorts**, 85 West Street - 212 385 4900
★ **Marriott Hotels & Resorts**, 1535 Broadway - 212 385 4900
★ **New York Palace Hotel**, 455 Madison Avenue - 212 888 7000
★ **Omni Berkshire**, 16 E 52nd Street - 212 888 4705
★ **Peninsula New York Hotel**, 700 5th Avenue - 212 956 2888
★ **Plaza Hotel**, 768 5th Avenue - 212 759 3000
★ **Radisson Hotel NY East Side**, 511 Lexington Avenue - 212 755 4400
★ **Regent Wall Street Hotel**, 55 Wall Street - 212 845 8600
★ **Ritz Tower**, 465 Park Avenue - 212 755 5000
★ **Ritz-Carlton San Juan**, 444 Madison Avenue - 212 813-9514
★ **Ritz-Carlton New York-Central Park**, 50 Central Park S - 212 308 9100
★ **Sofitel Hotels International**, 420 Lexington Avenue - 212 286 4108
★ **St Regis**, 2 E 55th Street - 212 753 4500
★ **St Regis Essex House**, 160 Central Park S - 212 247 0300
★ **Trump International Hotel**, 1 Central Park W - 212 299 1000

## Language school work

★ **American Language Institute**, 48 Cooper Square - 212 998 7040
★ **Berlitz Language Center**, 2 Rector Street - 212 766 2388
★ **English Conversation Classes**, 216 45th Street - 212 867 8700
★ **Language Workshop for Children**, 888 Lexington Avenue - 212 936 1369
★ **New York Language Center**, 2637 Broadway - 212 678 5800

**north east coast**

# new york

## Office work

★ **Accountemps**, 565 Fifth Avenue, 12th Floor - 212 687 7878, new.york.midtown@accountemps.com, www.accountemps.com

★ **AccuStaff**, 489 Fifth Avenue, 5th Floor - 212 687 8605, www.accustaff.com

★ **Adecco Employment Services**, Suite 501, 551 Fifth Avenue - 212 682 3438, ny.mt.ny@adecco.com, www.adecco.com

★ **Atrium**, 420 Lexington Avenue, Suite1410 - 212 292 0550, www.atriumstaff.com

★ **Core Staffing Services**, 59 John Street, 8th Floor - 212 766 1222, jsung@coretemps.com, www.coretemps.com

★ **CTI Personnel Group,** 331 Madison Avenue - 212 697 4000, ctipersonnel@cti-group.com, www.cti-group.com

★ **Eden Temporary Service**, 280 Madison Avenue - 212 685 4666

★ **Interim Personnel**, 545 Fifth Avenue - 212 983 8800, www.interim.com

★ **Kelly Temporary Services,** 420 Lexington Avenue - 212 949 8545, www.kellyservices.com

★ **Manpower**, 161 Avenue of Americas - 212 307 1008, www.manpower.com

★ **Manpower**, 111 Broadway - 212 406 4500, www.manpower.com

★ **Monster.com** - 312 782 3113, www.monster.com

★ **Olsten Staffing Services**, 500 Fifth Avenue - 212 391 7000, olsten@worldnet.att.net, www.olsten.com

★ **Personnel New York**, 90 Park Avenue - 212 351 5031, www.personnelnewyork.com

★ **Sloan Staffing Services**, 317 Madison Avenue - 212 949 7200, job@aolsloanstaff.com

★ **Staff Innovators**, 310 Madison Avenue - 212 490 7788, www.edenstaffing.com

★ **Staff Mark**, 420 Lexington Avenue - 212 271 3900, www.progressiveinfo.com

★ **Temporarily Yours Personnel Service**, 505 Fifth Avenue - 212 661 4850, staffing@tempyours.com, www.tempyours.com

★ **Today's Temporary**, 15 E 40th Street - 212 889 3232, www.todays.com

★ **Winston Resouces**, 535 Fifth Avenue - 212 687 5138, winstonet@aol.com

## Volunteer usher work

If you like the sound of free seats at some of the best shows in town and a chance to meet the great American public up close, then why not volunteer as an usher at one of New York's many theatres? All they ask is that you're on time, reasonably smart and that you're prepared to take people's tickets, tell them where the toilets are and generally make yourself useful. Bear in mind that we said volunteering, so expect nothing more than the pleasure of seeing some of New York's (and the world's) best shows for free in return for your work.

★ **Atlantic Theater Company**, 336 W 20th Street & 8th & 9th Avenues - 212 691 5919

★ **Blue Man Group, Astor Place Theatre**, 434 Lafayette Street (between Astor Place & E 4th Street) - 212 387 9415

★ **Cabaret**, Studio 54, 254 W 54th Street (between Broadway & 8th Avenue) - 212 239 6200

★ **Cherry Lane Theatre**, 38 Commerce Street (at 7th Avenue South) - 212 989 2020

★ **New York Theatre Workshop**, 79 E 4th Street (between 2nd & 3rd Avenues) - 212 780 9037

★ **Pearl Theatre Company**, Theatre 80, 80 St Marks Place (between 1st & 2nd Avenues) - 212 598 9802

★ **Performance Space 122**, 150 First Avenue (at 9th Street) - 212 477 5829

★ **Second Stage Theatre**, 307 W 43rd Street (between 8th & 9th Avenues) - 212 787 8302

★ **Vineyard Theatre**, 108 E 15th Street (at Union Square East) - 212 353 3366

## Other volunteering work

★ **Central Park Conservancy** - 212 360 2752, volunteer@centralparknyc.org, www.centralparknyc.org.

★ **Gay Men's Health Crisis** - 212 367 1000, www.gmhc.org

★ **Neighborhood Cats** - 212 662 5761, headcat@neighborhoodcats.org, www.neighborhoodcats.org

★ **New York Botanical Garden** - 718 817 8564, www.nybg.org

★ **Prospect Park Alliance** - 718 965 8960, www.prospectpark.org

★ **Queens Botanical Garden** - 718 886 3800, www.queensbotanical.org

# new york

**north east coast**

## Communications

### Internet cafés

★ **Cyber Café**, 250 W 49th Street between Broadway & 8th Avenue - 212 333 4109, www.cyber-cafe.com

★ **Easy Everything**, 234 W 42nd Street between 7th & 8th Avenues - 212 398 0775

★ **Internet Café**, 82 E 3rd Street between 1st & 2nd Avenues - 212 614 0747

★ **New York Public Library**, Science, Industry & Business Library, 188 Madison Avenue between 34th & 35th Streets - 212 592 7000, www.nypl.org

★ **NYC Wireless** - www.nycwireless.net (183 nodes in the city for free wireless access)

★ **Starbucks** - www.starbucks.net

### Postal services

★ **Express Mail** - 800 275 8777

★ **General Delivery**, 390 9th Avenue at 30th Street - 212 330 3099

★ **General Post Office**, 421 8th Avenue at 33rd Street - 800 275 8777

★ **Poste Restante**, General Post Office, 421 8th Avenue, attn: Window 29, New York, NY 10001

### Libraries

★ **Donnell Library Center**, 20 W 53rd Street between Fifth & Sixth Avenue - 212 621 0618, www.nypl.org

★ **Humanities & Social Sciences Library**, 455 Fifth Avenue at 42nd Street - 212 869 8089, www.nypl.org

★ **Library for the Performing Arts**, Lincoln Center, 111 Amsterdam Avenue between 65th & 66th Streets - 212 870 1630, www.nypl.org.

## Emergencies

### Police
★ **Emergency** - dial 911
★ **General information** - 646 610 5000 or 718 610 5000

### Hospitals
★ **Bellevue Hospital**, 462 1st Avenue at 27th Street - 212 562 4141
★ **Cabrini Medical Center**, 227 E 19th Street (between 2nd & 3rd Avenues) - 212 995 6000
★ **Columbia-Presbyterian Medical Center**, 168th Street & Broadway - 212 305 2500
★ **Mount Sinai Hospital**, Madison Avenue at 100th Street - 212 241 7171
★ **New York University Medical Center**, 34th Street & 1st Avenue - 212 263 5857
★ **Roosevelt Hospital**, 1000 Tenth Avenue at 59th Street - 212 523 6800
★ **St Luke's-Roosevelt Hospital**, 115th Street & Amsterdam - 212 523 4000
★ **St Vincent's Hospital**, 153 W 11th Street at 7th Avenue - 212 604 7998

## Consulates

**British Consulate-General in New York**
▤ 845 Third Avenue
☎ 212 745 0200
🏛 www.britain-info.org

**Consulate General of Ireland**
▤ 345 Park Avenue, 17th Floor
☎ 212 319 2562
🖱 conenny@aol.com

# philadelphia

## Why Philadelphia?

Philly prides itself on being the birthplace of modern America, the place where the Declaration of Independence was signed, the Constitution written and the Liberty Bell struck. But the city doesn't just dwell in the past - cutting edge clubs and bars make it a cool place to go out in. There are great shops, bars and restaurants and plenty to keep you occupied in the city's huge Fairmount Park - especially if you need to relax after all the historical sight-seeing. Even though it's a big place, Philly is a warm and welcoming city to live and work in. There's no arguing that life in one of America's largest cities is rich, diverse and always on the move.

## Some Philadelphia facts...

★ Philadelphia was the first place where the term 'The United States of America' was used.
★ It's the fifth largest city in the US and the second largest on the East Coast
★ Philadelphia has a population of 1.4 million.
★ 'The City of Brotherly Love' was founded in 1682 by English Quaker William Penn.
★ The Constitution of the United States was written in Philadelphia.

## Top things to do in Philadelphia...

★ Educate your ear at Zanzibar Blue (downstairs at the Bellvue, Broad & Walnut Streets). It's well known for 'the hottest jazz in town' and you can see (and hear) why. Go during the week to see some local talent (the musical kind) and on weekends for big-time players. They also do a good jazz brunch on Sundays.
★ Spend some time in the Independence National Historical Park, 'America's most historic square mile'. There's Liberty Bell (a bell), Independence Hall (a hall) and a huge amount of American history in between. Independence Hall is where colonists adopted Thomas Jefferson's Declaration of Independence on 4 July 1776 - just a little bit important, then...
★ Get involved in some real city life on South Street - great for nightlife and equally great for day life. Go party! Go shop!

## Philadelphia Convention & Visitors Bureau

▤ 1515 John F Kennedy Boulevard (at 16th Street)
☎ 800 537 7676
⌂ www.pcvb.org

## Getting there

Philadelphia International Airport is seven miles from the city centre. A lot of international airlines use Philly as a gateway to other American cities so it's fairly busy. The best way to get to the city centre is to take the high speed rail line. The train runs from 5.25am and stops when the last flight arrives at 11.25pm. It costs $5.50.

There are also airport buses and taxis but bear in mind that a taxi from the airport to the city centre costs around $20.

If you're getting into Philly by bus you need to know that the Greyhound bus station is on 11th Filbert Street. The Amtrak railway station is further along on 30th Street.

## Getting around

The Southern Pennsylvania Transportation System (SEPTA) is responsible for Philadelphia's public transport including a subway covering the city centre area. And there's buses and rail for anywhere else. Check out the SEPTA website for more information about the fares and routes...

 www.septa.org

# philadelphia

## Accommodation

## Hostels

★ **HI-Bank Street Hostel**, 32 South Bank Street - 215 922 0222
★ **HI-Chamounix Mansion Philadelphia**, Chamounix Drive, West Fairmont Park - 215 878 3676

## Work

Philadelphia is quickly shedding the industrial past that gave it its grim, hard working image. Ever seen 'Rocky'? Philadelphia was not a pretty place in the mid-seventies, but now skyscrapers dot the skyline and new businesses and new technologies have brought money and jobs to this great city. Philadelphia is still a place for hard work but everybody is enjoying themselves a lot more.

## Bar work

★ **Bridget Foy's**, 200 South Street - 215 922 1813
★ **Bridgid's**, 726 N 24th Street - 215 232 3232
★ **Cavanaugh's**, 119 S 39th Street - 215 386 4889
★ **City Tavern**, 138 Second - 215 413 1443
★ **Dawson Street Pub**, 100 Dawson, Manayunk - 215 482 5677
★ **Dickens Inn**, 421 S Second Street - 215 928 9307
★ **Eulogy Belgian Tavern**, 136 Chestnut Street - 215 413 2354
★ **Fado Irish Pubs**, 1500 Locust Street - 215 893 9700
★ **Fergie's Pub**, 1214 Sansom Street - 215 928 8118
★ **The Grey Lodge Pub**, 6235 Frankford Avenue - 215 624 2969
★ **The Irish Bards**, 2013 Walnut Street - 215 569 9585
★ **London Grill**, 23rd & Fairmount - 215 978 4545
★ **McGillin's Old Ale House**, 1310 Drury Lane - 215 735 5562
★ **McMenamin's**, 7170 Germantown Avenue - 215 247 9920
★ **Monk's Cafe**, 263 S 16th Street - 215 545 7005
★ **Moriarty's**, 1116 Walnut Street - 215 627 7676
★ **Standard Tap**, 901 North 2nd Street (2nd & Poplar) - 215 238 0630
★ **Tavern on Green**, 2047 Green Street - 215 235 6767

## Hotel work

- ★ **Courtyard by Marriott - Philadelphia Airport**, 8900 Bartram Avenue - 215 365 2200
- ★ **Embassy Suites Philadelphia Center City**, 1776 Benjamin Franklin Parkway - 215 561 1776
- ★ **Four Points Hotel Philadelphia Airport,** 4101 Island Avenue - 215 492 0400
- ★ **Four Seasons Hotel**, One Logan Square (18th Street & Benjamin Franklin Parkway) - 215 963 1500, www.fourseasons.com
- ★ **Hilton Garden Inn - Philadelphia City Center**, 1100 Arch Street - 215 923 0100
- ★ **Hilton Inn at Penn**, 3600 Sansom Street - 215 222 0200, www.HiltonInnAtPenn.com
- ★ **Hawthorn Suites** Phildelphia at the Convention Center, 1100 Vine Street - 215 829 8300
- ★ **Kormansuites Hotel**, 2001 Hamilton Street - 215 569 7200
- ★ **Omni Hotel at Independence Park**, 401 Chestnut Street - 215 925 0000
- ★ **Penn's View Hotel**, 14 N Front Street - 215 922 7600, www.pennsviewhotel.com
- ★ **Philadelphia Marriott**, 1201 Market Street - 215 625 2900
- ★ **Ritz Carlton Philadelphia**, 10 Avenue Of The Arts - 215 735 7700
- ★ **Wyndham Philadelphia At Franklin Plaza**, North 17th Street at Race Street - 215 448 2000

## Language school work

- ★ **Avente Tutoring**, 8012 Castor Avenue - 215 425 0100
- ★ **Berlitz Language Center**, 1608 Walnut Street - 215 735 8500
- ★ **Drexel English Language Center**, 229 N 33rd Street - 215 895 2022

**north east coast**

# philadelphia

## Office work

★ **Adecco Employment Services**, 1760 Market Street - 215 567 2390, info@adeccona.com, www.USAdecco.com
★ **American Staffing Resources (Office & Labor)**, 7201 Frankford Avenue - 215 333 7337
★ **Elitemps**, 1515 Market Street - 215 564 4884, www.judieliot.com
★ **Kelly Services**, 1635 Market Street - 215 564 3110
★ **Millennium Staffing**, 2005 Market Street - 215 988 1700
★ **Office Team**, 1735 Market Street - 215 568 0461
★ **Randstad**, 2 Penn Center - 215 569 3737
★ **Remedy Temporaries,** 30 South 15th Street - 215 665 8040
★ **Snelling Personnel Services**, 1617 John F Kennedy Boulevard - 215 568 1414, philadelphia@snellingeast.com
★ **Stivers Temporary Personnel**, 1 Penn Center - 215 561 1355
★ **TAC Temps**, 1617 John F Kennedy Boulevard - 215 568 4466
★ **United Temps**, 5070 Whitaker Avenue - 215 831 8151
★ **Westaff** - 215 564 1516

## Communications

## Libraries

★ **Bushroad Library**, 6304 Castor Avenue - 215 685 1471
★ **Chestnut Hill Library**, 8711 Germantown Avenue - 215 248 0977
★ **The Free Library of Philadelphia**, 1901 Vine Street - 215 686 5322
★ **West Philadelphia Regional Library**, 125 S 52nd Street - 215 823 7424

## Emergencies

**Pennsylvania Hospital**
✉ 2 Franklin Town Boulevard
☎ 215 988 4750

**City of Philadelphia Police Department**
✉ One Franklin Square
☎ 215 686 1776

# washington dc

## Why Washington DC?

The nation's capital was designed on a grand scale, with great leafy avenues and city planning inspired by Paris. It is a real cultural hotspot, with loads of free museums, concerts and art galleries, as well some of the USA's most famous buildings and monuments. The White House, the Vietnam Veteran's Memorial and the Holocaust Museum are among the countless places worth visiting in this spectacular city. There are plenty of job opportunities in Washington as well and with lots to keep you occupied when you're not working, the capital is a great place to live.

## Some Washington DC facts...
★ The White House was once burned down by British soldiers.
★ The 'DC' stands for 'District of Colombia'.
★ Washington National Cathedral is the sixth largest cathedral in the world.

## Top things to do in Washington DC...
★ Visit the United States Holocaust Memorial Museum and trace the story of Jewish persecution under the Nazi regime from its beginnings in 1933 to liberation in 1945.
★ You can spend ages in Union Station without even waiting for a train. As well as the Amtrak train and Metro subway stations, there are also shops, restaurants and a nine screen cinema - sorry, 'movie complex'.
★ Wander through the Arlington National Cemetery to see the graves of John F Kennedy, Robert Kennedy and Jacqueline Kennedy Onassis.
★ How about a free (yeah!) guided tour of the US Capitol, the seat of the legislative branch of the United States' government. See where it all happens.
★ Sneak off to the International Spy Museum and you too can find out more about the craft, practice, history and contemporary role of espionage. Ssshhh, don't mention it to anyone.

## Washington DC Convention and Tourism Corporation
 1212 New York Avenue, NW, Suite 600
☎ 202 789 7000
🏛 www.washington.org

# washington dc

## Getting there

Washington Dulles International Airport is 25 miles out of Washington DC but MetroRail has a direct connection between the airport and the city. The journey takes about 30 minutes. If you prefer travelling by bus, you can take the Washington Flyer coach which runs every 30 minutes.

Arriving by train is also worth a thought. The Old Union railway station in Washington is a sight itself - this amazing 90 year old building is on Massachusetts Avenue. Finally, if you are arriving by bus, the Greyhound bus terminal is on 1005 1st Street. For queries about timetables or fares visit Greyhound's website...

    www.greyhound.com

## Getting around

Washington public transport (regional bus system and the subway) is looked after by WMATA. But the easiest way to get around is definitely the subway. A one day pass is $6 and a seven day pass is $20. If you're wanting to travel a bit further out of the city centre, go for the Metro Bus. A one way ticket is $1.20 and a weekly bus pass is $11

    www.wmata.com

## Accommodation

## Hostels

★    **Allen Lee Hotel**, 2224 F Street NW - 202 331 1224
★    **American Guest House,** 1700 Sherwood Hall Lane - 703 768 0335
★    **HI-Washington DC,** 1009 11th Street, NW - 202 737 2333, reserve@hiwashingtondc.org, www.hiwashingtondc.org
★    **India House Too DC**, 300 Carroll Street - 202 291 1195, Rigsbie@hotmail.com, www.dchostel.com
★    **International Student Center DC**, 2451 18th Street, NW - 202 667 7681
★    **Norwich Hostel**, 4607 Norwich Road, College Park, MD 20740 - 240 472 2572

# washington dc

## Work

The administrative capital of the USA is a natural magnet for people of all kinds and the service industry that provides for them is always looking for extra workers. As well as the government-related temporary jobs, Washington also has plenty of opportunities for people who want to work in the supporting businesses. You can be one of the people who make their sandwiches or serve them their drinks after a hard day running the country.

## Bar work

★ **Brickskeller**, 1523 22nd Street, NW - 202 293 1885
★ **Cafe Berlin**, 322 Massachusetts Avenue NE - 202 543 7656
★ **Capitol Lounge**, 229-231 Pennsylvania - 202 542 098
★ **Colonel Brook's Tavern**, 901 Monroe Street - 202 529 4002
★ **The Dubliner**, 520 N Capitol - 202 737 3772
★ **Four Provinces**, 3421 Connecticut Avenue - 202 244 0860
★ **Kelly's Irish Times**, 14 F Street NW - 202 543 5433
★ **Murphy's Grand Irish Pub**, 713 King Street - 703 548 1717
★ **Murphy's Irish Pub**, 2605 24th Street - 202 462 7171
★ **Montgomery Grille**, 7200 Wisconsin Avenue, Bethesda - 301 654 3595
★ **My Brother's Place**, 237 Second Street NW - 202 347 1350
★ **Old Europe**, 2434 Wisconsin Avenue NW - 202 333 7600
★ **RFD Washington (Regional Food & Drink)**, 810 Seventh Street NW - 202 289 2030
★ **The Big Hunt**, 1345 Connecticut Avenue - 202 785 2333
★ **The Tombs**, 1226 36th Street NW - 202 337 6668

# washington dc

## Hotel work

- ★ **Best Western Capitol Skyline Hotel**, South Cap & I Streets Southwest - 202 488 7500
- ★ **Best Western Downtown Capital Hill**, 724 3rd Street Northwest - 202 842 4466
- ★ **Capitol Hilton**, 16th & K Streets Northwest - 202 393 1000
- ★ **Grand Hyatt Washington**, 1000 H Street Northwest - 202 582 1234
- ★ **Hyatt Regency Washington On Capitol Hill**, 400 New Jersey Avenue Northwest - 202 737 1234
- ★ **Madison**, 15th & M Streets NW - 202 862 1600
- ★ **Marriott**, 1221 22nd Street NW - 202 872 1500
- ★ **Marriott at Metro Center**, 775 12th Street Northwest - 202 737 2200
- ★ **Mayflower Hotel**, 1127 Connecticut Avenue NW - 202 347 3000
- ★ **Park Hyatt Washington**, 24th At M Street Northwest - 202 466 4326
- ★ **St Gregory Luxury Hotel & Suites**, 2033 M Street NW - 202 530 3600
- ★ **State Plaza Hotel**, 2117 E Street NW - 202 861 8200
- ★ **Washington Courtyard**, 1900 Connecticut Avenue Northwest - 202 332 9300
- ★ **Westin Grand Hotel**, 2350 M Street NW - 202 429 0100
- ★ **Willard Inter Continental Hotel**, 1401 Pennsylvania Avenue Northwest - 202 628 9100
- ★ **Wyndham City Center**, 1143 New Hampshire Avenue Northwest - 202 775 0800

# washington dc

## Office work

- ★ **AA Temps**, 1730 K Street Northwest Suite 307 - 202 955 6100, info@ardelle.com
- ★ **Adecco Employment Services**, 1300 Connecticut Avenue Northwest - 202 857 0800, info@adeccona.com, www.USAdecco.com
- ★ **Ameritemps**, 818 Connecticut Avenue Northwest - 202 822 8003
- ★ **Answer Temps**, 910 17th Street Northwest - 202 835 0190
- ★ **Careerworld Tempworld Downtown**, 1050 17th Street Northwest - 202 296 7530
- ★ **Doyle Temps**, 1140 Connecticut Avenue Northwest - 202 296 3189
- ★ **Graham Staffing Service**, 1130 Connecticut Avenue NW - 202 861 1260, www.grahaminc.com
- ★ **Kelly Services**, 1850 M Street Northwest - 202 331 8383
- ★ **Manpower**, 1130 Connecticut Avenue Northwest - 202 331 8300
- ★ **Preferred Temporary Services**, 1600 K Street Northwest - 202 429 5637
- ★ **Randstad**, 1100 New York Avenue NW - 202 289 6566
- ★ **Snelling Personnel Services**, 1000 16th Street NW Ste 805 - 202 223 3540, jobs@snellingdc.com, www.snellingdc.com
- ★ **Temporaries Now** - 703 914-9100, www.temporariesnow.com
- ★ **Temporary Solutions** - 703 883 2291, jobs@tsijobs.com, www.tsijobs.com
- ★ **Temporary Staffing**, 1150 17th Street - 202 466 8230
- ★ **Temps & Co**, The Hill - 202 393 2388
- ★ **Westaff,** 1101 Connecticut Avenue Northwest - 202 293 7333

## Language school work

- ★ **Berlitz Language Center**, 1050 Connecticut Avenue - 202 331 1160
- ★ **Center for Innovative Language**, 320 Independence Avenue - 202 544 0888
- ★ **International Language Institute**, 4301 Connecticut Avenue - 202 362 2505
- ★ **Languageone**, 2305 Calvert Street - 202 328 0099

# washington dc

## Communications

## Internet café
★ **CyperSTOP.café**, 1513 17th Street - 202 234 2470

## Libraries
★ **Columbia Public Library**, 901 6 Street - 202 001 4531
★ **Martin Luther King Memorial Library**, 9th in 6th Street NW - 202 727 0321
★ **Anacostia Branch Library**, 1800 Good Hope Road at 18th Street SW - 202 689 1190
★ **Cleveland Park Beach Library**, 3310 Connecticut Avenue NW - 202 282 3080

## Emergencies

**British Embassy**
✉ 3100 Massachusetts Avenue
☎ 202 588 7800

**DC General Hospital**
✉ 19th Massachusetts Avenue
☎ 202 698 5000

**Metropolitan Police Department**
✉ John A Wilson Building, 1350 Pennsylvania Avenue
☎ 202 727 1000

From Memphis to Miami and Nashville to New Orleans, the South has more than its fair share of America's most exciting cities. The South is staggeringly culturally rich - Cajun and Creole food, the blues, jazz, country and rock & roll were all born in the area. The place is (quite rightly) a mecca for anyone who likes good food and good music. The area also has an amazing history - from the birth of the Civil Rights movement to the shenannigans in Florida during the last Presidential election, it has been the scene of some of the most defining and dramatic moments in modern American history.

image courtesy of New Orleans Convention & Visitors Bureau

# atlanta

## Why Atlanta?

Atlanta is a city that has produced some of the most famous icons of the modern age, from Martin Luther King to Coca Cola. And now this thriving city is busy creating new ones, as a centre for big business and commercial innovation. Atlanta has managed to develop into a cosmopolitan and modern city, while keeping its very own strong Southern atmosphere and culture. The high quality of life, the grand scale and imaginative development of the city and the friendliness of the people make Atlanta a great place to be.

## Some Atlanta facts...
★ Coca Cola was launched in Atlanta in 1886.
★ Atlanta has a city population of more than 400,000.
★ The tallest hotel in the US is in Atlanta.

## Top things to do in Atlanta...
★ Visit the 21-acre Centennial Olympic Park, home of the 1996 Olympic Games, and imagine yourself up there on the podium...
★ See a summer film ('movie') or ballet at the Fox Theatre (660 Peachtree Street - 404 817 8700). Apparently the theatre is a Moorish, Egyptian, Art Deco fantasy!
★ Enjoy 'an oasis of beauty and tranquility' - no, not an hour relaxing in the bath but an afternoon in the Atlanta Botanical Garden. As well as the usual display gardens, there's a 15-acre hardwood forest with walking trails.
★ A trip to Atlanta is not complete without visiting the World of Coca-Cola. You too can learn that an average of 9,600 Coca-Cola Company beverages are consumed every second. Amazing (burp!).
★ Find at more about Martin Luther King and the Civil Rights Movement at the Martin Luther King Jr Historic Site - films, exhibits, guides and a bookstore to help get you up to speed.
★ Soak it all up at Blind Willie's, one of Atlanta's top rated Blues clubs. Major artists perform on a regular basis and the club is open everyday.

## Atlanta Convention & Visitors Bureau
233 Peachtree Street NE, Suite 100
404 521 6600
www.acvb.com

## Getting there

The Metropolitan Atlanta Rapid Transit Authority (MARTA) runs a scheduled service to and from Hartsfield Atlanta International Airport. The MARTA entrance is via the west entrance of the terminal complex. MARTA trains arrive and depart from the airport every 8 minutes on a 15 minute journey to downtown Atlanta.

   www.itsmarta.com

Shared-Ride Shuttles depart every 10 to 15 minutes during flight hours.

If you're arriving by bus, the Greyhound bus station is at 232 Forsyth Street.

## Getting around

Rail cars and buses are Atlanta's public transport options. The MARTA system has 36 stations, 700 buses and 235 rail cars. A single fare is $1.75, a weekly TransCard is $13 and a monthly TransCard is $52.50. MARTA also does a student pass for $10.

   www.itsmarta.com

## Accommodation

## Hostel

★   **Atlanta International Hostel**, 223 Ponce De Leon Avenue - 404 872 1042

south & florida

# atlanta

## Work

A great standard of living and fantastic employment opportunities make Atlanta a good choice for anyone wanting to live in the Southern states. Coca-Cola isn't the only big player in Atlanta, and the city has a diverse and dynamic business community that is always looking to recruit new people.

## Bar & restaurant work

★ **Atkins Park Restaurant**, 794 N Highland Avenue - 404 876 7249
★ **Beer Mug Lounge**, 857 Collier Road Northwest - 404 603 9601
★ **Chucks Clubhouse Neighborhood Pub**, 1995 Windy Hill Road Southeast - 770 319 6641
★ **Club Enigma**, 265 E Paces Ferry Road - 404 264 8824
★ **Derby Food & Spirits**, 1155 Hammond Drive Northeast - 770 396 8808
★ **Famous Pub & Sports Palace**, 2947 North Druid Hills Road Northeast - 404 633 3555
★ **Frogs Cantina**, 931 Monroe Drive Northeast - 404 607 9967
★ **The Gate Sports Bar & Grill**, 2505 Godby Road - 404 761 3921
★ **Jocks & Jills & Frankie's Sports Grill**, 5600 Roswell Road - 770 209 0920
★ **Mardi Gras**, 6300 Powers Ferry Road Northwest - 770 955 1638
★ **Midtown Saloon & Grill**, 736 Ponce De Leon Avenue Northeast - 404 874 1655
★ **Okiahs Sports Bar & Grill**, 4335 Roosevelt Highway - 404 763 5047
★ **Olde Bailey**, 777 Ponce De Leon Avenue Northeast - 770 638 3223
★ **Park Tavern**, 500 10th Street - 404 249 0001
★ **Pete's Sports Bar & Grill**, 6600 Roswell Road Northeast - 404 943 0463
★ **Rico's View On Ponce**, 736 Ponce De Leon Avenue Northeast - 404 873 3220
★ **Sambuca Jazz Café**, 3102 Piedmont Road Northeast - 404 237 5299

# atlanta

## Hotel work

★ **Hawthorn Suites**, 1500 Parkwood Cir Se - 770 952 9595
★ **Hilton Atlanta Airport & Towers**, 1031 Virginia Avenue - 404 767 9000
★ **Hilton Atlanta Northwest**, 2055 South Park Place Southeast - 770 953 9300
★ **Hilton Atlanta & Towers**, 255 Courtland Street Northeast - 404 659 2000
★ **Hilton Hotels - Peachtree Corners**, 5993 Peachtree Industrial - 770 447 4747
★ **Hilton Hotels - Northwest**, 1031 Virginia Avenue - 770 953 9300
★ **Radisson Hotel**, 165 Courtland Street Northeast - 404 581 9658
★ **Ramada Inn & Conference Center**, 418 Armour Drive Northeast - 404 873 4661
★ **Regency Suites Hotel**, 975 Peachtree Street Northeast - 404 876 5003
★ **Renaissance Atlanta Hotel Concourse**, 1 Hartsfield Center Park - 404 209 9999
★ **Renaissance Atlanta Hotel Downtown**, 590 West Peachtree Street Northwest - 404 881 6000
★ **Ritz Carlton**, 181 Peachtree Street Northeast - 404 659 0400
★ **Sheraton Atlanta Hotel**, 165 Courtland Street - 404 659 6500
★ **Swissotel Atlanta**, 3391 Peachtree Road Northeast - 404 365 0065
★ **The Westin Atlanta North**, 7 Concourse Parkway - 770 395 3900
★ **The Westin Atlanta Airport**, 4736 Best Road - 404 762 7676
★ **Wyndham Atlanta**, 160 Spring Street Northwest - 404 688 8600

# atlanta

## Office work

★ **Allstaff**, 1955 Cliff Valley Way Northeast - 404 633 8280

★ **Atlanta Temporary Staffing**, 1266 Moreland Avenue Southeast - 404 635 1717

★ **DCCA Professional Temporaries**, 5 Concourse Parkway Northeast - 770 395 0014

★ **Horizon Staffing**, 3631 Chamblee Tucker Road - 770 938 3138

★ **Manpower**, 591 Thornton Road - 770 497 9675

★ **Officeteam - Atlanta Downtown**, 133 Peachtree Street Northeast - 404 523 8823

★ **Quest Temporary Services**, 1475 Atlanta Industrial West - 404 699 7447

★ **Randstad**, 2200 Northlake Parkway, Tucker - 770 491 1222

★ **Selective Staffing Services**, 4151 Memorial Drive - 770 497 9958

★ **Temp Choice**, 5150 Buford Highway Northeast - 770 447 4199

★ **Temp Resources**, 34 Peachtree Street Northwest - 404 659 9400

★ **Tempworld - Marietta Cumberland**, 3350 Riverwood Parkway Southeast - 770 916 1889

★ **TMD Temporaries**, 2581 Piedmont Road Northeast - 404 264 1988

★ **Today's Temporary**, 200 Galleria Parkway Southeast - 770 953 8002

★ **Vision 2000 Temporary Services**, 2785 Clairmont Road Northeast - 404 636 1992

★ **Will Staff Temporaries**, 5328 Glenridge Drive Northeast - 404 250 1391

# Internet cafés

★   **Innovox: A Connectivity Lounge**, 699 Ponce de Leon Avenue, Suite 1 - 404 872 4482, innovox@aol.com, www.innovoxlounge.com

★   **Maasty Computers Internet Café**, 736A Ponce De Leon Avenue NE - 404 294 8095, www.maastyinternetcafe.com

★   **Red Light Café**, 553 Amsterdam Avenue - redlight@mindspring.com

# Emergencies

### British Consulate-General
✉   Georgia Pacific Centre, Suite 3400, 133 Peachtree Street NE
☎   404 954 7700
🖱   BritishConsulateGeneral.Atlanta@fco.gov.uk

### Atlanta Police Department
✉   675 Ponce de Leon Avenue
☎   404 853 3434

### St Joseph's Hospital
✉   5665 Peachtree Dunwoody Road
☎   404 851 7001

# austin

## Why Austin?

Austin is proof that there's much more to Texas than just cowboy hats, oil and big business. The city has an ever-expanding music scene and a reputation as a hang-out for students, intellectuals, artists, musicians and environmentalists. You'll hopefully experience good old fashioned Texan hospitality and friendliness. Students from the University of Texas as well as locals flock to the city's clubs and bars to listen to some of the best live music in the States. Austin's creative sparkle combined with Texan hard work and business acumen have made this a booming city and a great place to live and work.

## Some Austin facts...

★ Austin has an average of 300 days of sun a year.
★ The average age of people living in Austin is 29, compared with the national average of 34.
★ The city has the most bars and restaurants per capita in the USA.

## Top things to do in Austin...

★ Climb the 106 steps of Mt Bonnell to enjoy the great view.
★ Take a moonlight tour of the Wide Basion Preserve.
★ Walk, jog or bike the Hike and Bike Trail along Town Lake.
★ Explore Austin's historic cemeteries where Texas legends have been laid to rest.
★ View the unique late 19th-century Moonlight Tower.
★ Watch the UT Longhorns play at Memorial Stadium.
★ Spend a few hours experiencing rural central Texas as it was in the 1880s (smells and all) at the Jourdan-Bachman Pioneer Farm.

## Austin Convention & Visitors Bureau

✉ 201 E Second Street
☎ 800 926 2282
⌂ www.austintexas.org

## Getting there

Austin-Bengstrom Airport is 30 to 40 minutes away from Austin. Shuttle buses 100 and 350 run regularly from the first morning flight until the last one in the evening.

If you're coming in by train, Amtrak's railway station is a mile away from downtown on N Lamar Boulevard.

If you are arriving into the Greyhound bus station, it's at E Koenig Lane.

## Getting around

Austin public transport is efficient and reliable. A 20 ride booklet costs $5.00 and a monthly bus pass is only $10.00. For more information about the routes and fares visit CAP's website...

 www.capmetro.austin.tx.us

## Accommodation

## Hostels

★   **Hostelling International Austin**, 2200 S Lakeshire Boulevard - 512 444 2294, hostel@hiaustin.org

## Camping

★   **Austin Creek State Recreation Area** - 707 869 2015
★   **Austin Parks/Cedar Parks**, 500 Cedar Breaks Road - 512 258 4121

## Work

There are so many music venues, bars and restaurants looking for temporary workers in Austin, especially whenever the city's many festivals are on. As one of the South's major cultural centres, there are always events taking place, from film festivals to musical extravaganzas, and it's worth putting your name about and seeing if they can use you.

## Bar work

- ★ **Addle Bar**, 120 W 5th Street - 512 322 9291
- ★ **Antone's**, 213 W 5th Street - 512 474 5314
- ★ **Babes**, 208 E 6th, - 512 473 2262
- ★ **Barfly's**, 5420 Airport Boulevard - 512 452 6455
- ★ **BB Rover's Café & Pub**, 12636 Research Boulevard Ste B101, - 512 335 9504
- ★ **Bitter End**, 311 Colorado Street- 512 478 2337
- ★ **Blind Pig Pub**, 317 E 6th Street - 512 472 0809
- ★ **Broken Spoke**, 3201 S Lamar Boulevard - 512 442 6189
- ★ **Cedar Street**, 208 W Fourth - 512 708 8811
- ★ **Crown & Anchor Pub**, 2911 San Jacinto Boulevard - 512 322 9168
- ★ **Ego's**, 510 S Congress Avenue - 512 474 7091
- ★ **Elephant Room**, 315 Congress Avenue - 512 473 2279
- ★ **Emo's**, 603 Red River Street - 512 477 3667
- ★ **Fado Irish Pub**, 214 W 4th Street - 512 457 0172
- ★ **Friends**, 208 E 6th Street - 512 320 8193
- ★ **Ginger Man Pub**, 304 W 4th Street- 512 473 8801
- ★ **Green Parrot**, 124 N LBJ Drive - 512 396 4259
- ★ **Lovejoy's**, Goyneches Street - 512 477 1268
- ★ **Meno**, 217 Congress - 512 479 5094
- ★ **Mother Egan's Irish Pub**, 715 W 6th Street - 512 478 7747
- ★ **Mugshots**, 701 Congress Avenue - 512 457 8800
- ★ **Palmeras**, 217 Congress Avenue - 512 479 5002
- ★ **Raggedy Anne's**, 2113 Wells Branch - 512 251 9647
- ★ **Red Eyed Fly**, 715 Red River Street - 512 480 0171
- ★ **Steamboat**, 110 E Riverside - 512 707 2628
- ★ **Speakeasy**, 412D Congress Avenue - 512 476 8086

## Hotel work

★ **Austin B Central**, 7522 North IH-35 - 512 323 2121
★ **Austin Hills on Lake Travis**, 317 Ranch Road 620 S - 512 452 9391
★ **Best Western Seville Plaza Inn**, 4323 South Interstate Highway 35 - 512 447 5511
★ **Crown Plaza Hotel**, 500 N I H 35 - 512 480 8181
★ **Double Tree Hotel Austin**, 6505 North 1H-35 - 512 454 3737
★ **Governor's Inn**, 611 W 22nd Street - 512 477 0711
★ **Four Season Hotel**, 700 San Jacinto 8th Street - 512 478 4500
★ **Hyatt Regency Austin**, 208 Barton Springs - 512 477 1234
★ **Lake Austin Spa Resort**, 1705 S Quinlan Park Road - 512 372 7362
★ **North Park Executive Suite Hotel**, 7685 North Cross Drive - 512 452 9391
★ **Omni Austin Hotel**, 700 San Jacinto A 8th Street 512 476 3700
★ **Radisson Hotel & Suites**, 111 East Cesar Chaver Street - 512 478 9611
★ **Wellesley Inn & Suites Austin Town Lake**, 1001 S IH-35 - 512 326 0100

**south & florida**

## Office work

★ **Austin Personel**, 7514 N Mopal Suite 200, info@austinpersonel.com, www.jobaustin.com,
★ **Austin At Work** - 512 812 5907, www.austinatwork.com
★ **Austin Personnel Service**, 3307 Northland Drive Street 450 - 512 454 6822
★ **Accounts Temps**, 6836 Austin Centre Boulevard Street 120 - 512 345 0303
★ **Adecco Employment Service**, 3407 Wells Branch Street 890 - 512 452 9300
★ **Appleone Employment Service**, Wells Branch Street 575 - 512 238 1405
★ **All Temps Personel Service**, 1524 IH-355 Street 232 - 512 322 5146
★ **Corestaff**, 7800 N MoPac ExPy Street 320 - 512 345 1010
★ **Express Personnel**, 2107 N Mays Round Rock - 512 255 2525

★ **General Employment**, 1250 S. Capital of Tex Highway Street
265 - 512 347 8600
★ **Instaff Personnel Service**, 825 E Rundberg Lane Street H2 -
512 339 0777
★ **Interim Personnel Service**, 3910 iH-35S Street 235 -
512 443 9675

## Language schools

★ **Austin English Academy**, 1201 W 24th Suite 210 -
512 476 1933, www.austinenglishacademy.com
★ **Creative Language Center**, 1912 W Anderson Lane Suite 203A
- 512 453 8680

## Communications

**Austin Public Library**
✉ PO Box 1088
☎ 512 974 3324

## Emergencies

**Austin State Hospital**
✉ 4110 Guadalupe Street
☎ 512 324 842

**Brackenridge Hospital**
✉ 601 E 15th Street
☎ 512 324 842

**Main Police Department**
✉ PO Box 689001
☎ 512 974 5000

## Why Houston?

Over 90 different languages are spoken in this fast moving, culturally diverse city of nearly two million people. They all contribute to make Houston one of the most exciting cities in the US. Obviously there is a lot of oil money washing around in the city, and lots of big hats and big cars, but the city also has plenty of students, artists and young people just doing their thing. Business is always booming in Houston in one way or another, so there are plenty of temporary work and work experience options in this great southern city.

## Some Houston facts

★ 'Houston' was the first word that anybody said on the moon.
★ Two million people live within Houston's city limits.
★ Houston Grand Opera is the only opera company to have won a Tony, two Grammy awards and two Emmy awards.
★ Houston's Museum of Fine Arts is the sixth largest museum in the country.

## Top things to do in Houston

★ Have an 'out-of-this-world' experience (groan!) at SpaceCenter Houston. Interactive exhibits, IMAX films, live demos and tours of NASA's Johnson Space Center. Quite exciting really.
★ Wander around Moody Gardens (great name!) which also have an IMAX 3-D Theater, IMAX Ridefilm Theater, Discovery Museum, Rainforest Pyramid and Palm Beach recreation. www.moodygardens.com
★ Visit the Houston Museum of Natural Science which, although you'd think otherwise, is not a museum. It also houses Burke Baker Planetarium, IMAX Theater, Challenger Center, Strake Hall of Malacology and butterfly tropical rainforest. And there's more - the satellite facility has an observatory and there's a second Challenger Center.

**Greater Houston Convention & Visitors Bureau**
⊟ 901 Bagby, Suite 100
☎ 713 437 5200
🕸 www.houston-spacecityusa.com

# houston

## Getting there

Houston's two major airports are served by about 22 airlines between them. Make sure you check which airport you'll be arriving at because some airlines fly into both. George Bush Intercontinental Airport, 23 miles north of downtown Houston, is the city's international airport. And there's WP Hobby Airport - 7 miles south of downtown Houston for domestic flights.

Coach USA and Express Shuttle USA run a regular bus and shuttle service into Houston from George Bush Intercontinental. One way to downtown Houston is $19. For more phone...

☎    713 523 8888

The Houston Metropolitan Transit Authority (METRO) also has a bus service into town - you can catch it from the south side of Terminal C.

Amtrak trains arrive at the old Southern Pacific Station (902 Washington Avenue). And, if you're arriving by bus, Houston's Greyhound bus station is at 2121 Main Street.

## Getting around

Public transport in Houston is fairly well developed and reasonably priced. METRO operates an extensive bus service throughout the city from 5.00am until midnight. A one way bus fare in the city centre zone is $1.00 but more in other zones. You either buy tokens in advance or have the exact change to throw into the fare box. Day passes are $2 and weekly passes are $9...

    www.ridemetro.org

Houston parks are big on bike trails so you should seriously consider the bike option while you're there. You can hire a bike for $20 a day.

★    **West End Bicycles**, 5427 Blossom Street, east of Memorial Park - 713 861 2271

## Accommodation

### Hostels

★ **Houston International Hostel**, 5302 Crawford -
713 523 1009, resv@houstonhostel.com,
www.houstonhostel.com

### Work

You don't have to be into oil to get a job in Houston, as there are
hundreds of jobs going - this town always seems to be growing,
innovating and re-inventing itself.

### Bar & restaurant work

★ **Bubba's Sports Bar & Grill**, 6223 Washington Avenue -
713 861 7161
★ **Cockpit Bar & Grill**, 8101 Airport Boulevard - 713 640 2044
★ **Corner Bar & Grill**, 910 Temple Street - 713 862 0619
★ **Davenport**, 2115 Richmond Avenue - 713 520 1140
★ **Downing Street**, 2549 Kirby Drive - 713 523 2291
★ **Home Plate Bar & Grill**, 1800 Texas Street - 713 222 1993
★ **La Paloma Bar**, 6416 Wallisville Road - 713 672 2724
★ **Lost River Bar & Grill**, 7620 Katy Freeway - 713 680 2800
★ **Market Square Bar & Grill**, 311 Travis Street - 713 224 6133
★ **O'Malley's Irish Pub**, 2303 South Kirkwood Road -
281 556 5002
★ **Outback Pub**, 3100 Fountain View Drive - 713 780 2323
★ **Rays Ice House**, 7504 Lyons Avenue - 713 671 2020
★ **Sherlock's Baker Street Pub**, 10001 Westheimer Road -
713 977 1857
★ **Six Pack Inn**, 3818 Cavalcade Street - 713 674 3374
★ **Time Out Sports Bar & Grill**, 1400 Shepherd Drive -
713 863 8865
★ **Vickie's Bar & Grill**, 12214 Market Street Road - 713 451 4331
★ **Yorkshire Pub**, 17550 West Little York Road - 281 345 4228

# houston

## Hotel work

- ★ **Hilton Garden Hotel**, 15400 John F Kennedy Boulevard - 281 449 4148
- ★ **Hilton Garden Inn Houston Northwest**, 7979 Willow Chase Boulevard - 832 912 1000
- ★ **Hilton Houston Plaza**, 6633 Travis Street - 713 313 4000
- ★ **Hilton - Nassau Bay & Marina**, 3000 Nasa Road 1 - 281 333 9300
- ★ **Hilton - Southwest**, 6780 Southwest Freeway - 713 977 7911
- ★ **Houston Marriott**, 1750 West Loop South - 713 960 0111
- ★ **Hyatt Regency Houston**, 1200 Louisiana Street - 713 654 1234
- ★ **Radisson Hotel & Conference Center**, 9100 Gulf Freeway - 713 943 7979
- ★ **Radisson Suite Hotel Houston West**, 10655 Katy Freeway - 713 461 6000
- ★ **Ramada Inn Pasadena**, 114 Richey Street, Pasadena - 713 477 6871
- ★ **Ramada Inn South**, 1301 Nasa Road 1 - 281 488 0220
- ★ **Sheraton Hotel**, 3000 North Loop West - 713 688 0100
- ★ **Sheraton North Houston**, 15700 John F Kennedy Boulevard - 281 442 5100
- ★ **Sheraton Suites Houston Near The Galleri**, 2400 West Loop South - 713 586 2444
- ★ **Westin Galleria & Oaks Hotels the Westin Oaks**, 5011 Westheimer Road - 713 960 8100
- ★ **Wyndam Hotel**, 12400 Greenspoint Drive - 281 875 2222

## Office work

★ **Accountemps**, 654 North Sam Houston Parkway East - 281 591 0044

★ **Adecco Employment Services**, 18333 Egret Bay Boulevard - 281 333 2330

★ **Carlton Staffing**, 13101 Northwest Freeway - 713 329 9990

★ **Corestaff**, 12200 Northwest Freeway - 713 683 9320

★ **Dan Temps**, 1100 Nasa Road 1 - 281 333 5203

★ **Energytemps**, 3100 South Gessner Road - 713 952 3004

★ **Express Personnel Services**, 256 N Sam Houston Parkway East - 281 931 7100

★ **Kelly Services**, 2000 Bering Drive - 713 972 1151

★ **Manpower**, 14811 Saint Mary's Lane - 281 589 2090

★ **Memorial Temporary Staffing**, 8585 Commerce Park Drive - 713 271 1118

★ **Modern Temps**, 7015 West Tidwell Road - 713 462 2473

★ **Randstad**, 1111 Fannin Street - 713 571 8565

★ **Snelling Personnel Services**, 9990 Richmond Avenue - 713 783 6900

★ **Staff Force**, 13240 Hempstead Road - 713 690 9696

★ **Staffmark**, 5600 Northwest Central Drive - 713 934 9933

★ **Temp Digest**, 10101 Southwest Freeway - 713 541 2468

★ **Temp Houston**, 480 North Sam Houston Parkway East - 281 820 2425

★ **Temp-Plus**, 9601 Jones Road - 281 890 2220

★ **Temporary Connection**, 12012 Wickchester Lane - 281 493 4300

★ **Temporary Edge**, 11211 Katy Freeway - 713 973 8367

★ **Temporary Professionals**, 10575 Katy Freeway - 713 465 1507

★ **Temporary Staffing Services**, 722 Fairmont Parkway - 713 941 0616

★ **Tempus**, 6060 Richmond Avenue - 713 977 3780

★ **TMD Temporaries**, 16715 Longenbaugh Drive - 281 966 9090

**south & florida**

# houston

## Internet café

★ **PJ's Coffee & Tea,** 4321 Montrose Boulevard - 713 521 2002

## Emergencies

**British Consulate-General**
✉ Wells Fargo Plaza, 19th Floor, 1000 Louisiana, Suite 1900
☎ 713 659 6270

**Houston Police Department**
✉ 1200 Travis Street
☎ 713 222 3131

**Houston Shriners Hospital**
✉ 6977 Main Street
☎ 713 797 1616

## Why Miami?

There's a bit more to Miami and Florida than Don Johnson, Miami Vice, cheesy Hawaiian shirts and Disneyland. Miami's location has made it a meeting point for many cultures, and the city's multicultural nature makes for a great mix of food, music and entertainment. It's known for its lively bars, clubs and spectacular nightlife. The city's artistic and cultural scene is also growing fast and there is always something to go and see or do. The city is famous for its beaches and tropical feel, but Miami is also a centre for big business in the area. There are many opportunities for work here, especially in the tourist industry.

## Some Miami facts...

★ Miami is the biggest port in the world for cruise ships.
★ More than 10 million tourists a year come to Miami-Dade County.
★ Miami's South Beach is home to the celebrity-owned restaurants of Casa Salsa (Ricky Martin) and Lario's (Gloria Estefan).

## Top things to do in Miami...

★ Spend far too long doing some people-watching - if you're lucky you'll find international celebrities, literati and glitterati, musicians and more.
★ Go surfing at South Pointe Park, South Beach. Or just sit on the beach and pretend you know how to!
★ Absorb a bit of Art Deco in Miami's (wait for it) Art Deco District - 800 buildings in the distinctive architectural style of the 1930s. And if you're **really** interested, there's the Art Deco Welcome Center (1001 Ocean Drive - 305 672 2014) for info and tours.
★ Cuban Memorial Boulevard, in the heart of Little Havana, is lined with monuments commemorating the heroes that fought for Cuban independence. You can see the eternal flame that burns in memory of the 94 Cuban exiles who gave their lives in the foiled 1961 Bay of Pigs Invasion.
★ And don't forget about Miami Art Museum in the Metro-Dade Cultural Center. It has changing exhibitions from around the world and is building a permanent collection.

### Greater Miami Convention & Visitors Bureau

701 Brickell Avenue, Suite 2700

305 539 3000

www.gmcvb.com

**south & florida**

# miami

## Getting there

Miami International Airport is the second busiest airport in America so shuttle buses, taxis, airport buses and the metro-rail run frequently between the airport and city. The easiest way to get into Miami is to jump onto the metro. Just follow the signs at the airport and you're in central Miami before you know it.

The Greyhound bus station is in downtown Miami on 100 NW 6th Street. The Amtrak station is a bit further along on 8303 NW 37th Avenue on NW 79th Street.

## Getting around

Miami's public transport is split between the bus and rail system. The rail system links suburban Miami while the buses run around the city centre. A single ticket on the bus is $1.25.

You may even want to consider hiring a car or buying a cheap second-hand one if you're serious about getting around Miami. There are loads of car hire companies in the city centre but here's a few to start you off...

★ **Avis**, 2330 NW 37 Avenue - 305 341 0973
★ **Budget**, 3902 NW 28 Street - 305 871 3053
★ **Hertz**, 3795 NW 21 Street- 305 871 0300
★ **Florida Auto Rental**, 4021 NW 38 Street - 305 871 6032

## Hostels

★ **HI-Miami Beach International Hostel**, 1438 Washington Avenue - 305 534 2988
★ **Miami Beach International Travelers Hostel**, 236 9th Street - 305 534 0268
★ **The Tropics Hotel & Hostel**, 1550 Collins Avenue - 305 531 0361, mail@tropicshotel.com, www.tropicshotel.com

## Camping

★ **Lakry & Penny Thompson Park & Campground**, 12451 SW 184 Streets - 305 232 1049
★ **Miami Camp**, 8851 West 400N Frankton - 765 734 1365
★ **Miami Everglades KOA Campground**, 20675 SW 162nd Avenue - 305 233 5300

## Work

In between topping up your tan and dancing the night away, you're going to need a job in Miami. Here we've included details of some of the top places to get work, whether behind a bar or behind a desk.

## Bar work

★ **Abbey Brewing Co**, 115 16th Street, Miami Beach - 305 538 8110

★ **Astor Place Bar & Grill**, 956 Washington Avenue, Miami Beach - 305 672 7217

★ **Bolero Bar & Grill**, 661 Washington Avenue, Miami Beach - 305 673 6516, info@bolerosouthbeach.com

★ **Bolero Bar & Grill**, 4045 Sheridan Avenue, Miami Beach - 305 673 6516

★ **Champion's Sports Bar & Grill**, 4400 Northwest 87th Avenue - 305 591 6626

★ **Churchill's A Sort of English Pub**, 5501 Northeast 2nd Avenue - 305 757 1807

★ **Clevelander Bar**, 1020 Ocean Drive - 305 531 3485

★ **Doral Golf Resort & Spa - Champions' Sports Bar & Grill**, 4400 Northwest 87th Avenue - 305 591 6626

★ **Flanigan's Seafood Bar & Grill**, 12790 Southwest 88th Street - 305 380 0521

★ **Flanigan's Seafood Bar & Grill** - No 9, 1550 West 84th Street, Hialeah - 305 821 0993

★ **Flanigan's Seafood Bar & Grill** - No 20, 13205 Biscayne Boulevard - 305 893 0506

★ **Gables Pub**, 270 Catalonia Avenue - 305 476 1101

★ **Jam's Sports Bar**, 1331 Washington Avenue, Miami Beach - 305 532 6700

★ **Jimmy Johnson's Three Rings Bar**, 4525 Collins Avenue - 800 327 8337

★ **Shack**, 21855 South Dixie Highway - 305 258 0693

★ **Thai Orchid Restaurant & Brew Public**, 317 Miracle Mile - 305 443 6364

★ **Thirst & Ten Sports Bar,** 19201 Collins Avenue, Miami Beach - 305 932 2233

★ **Veranda Bar & Grill**, 1717 North Bayshore Drive - 305 372 1875

# miami

## Hotel work

★ **Alexander All Suite Oceanfront Resort**, 5225 Collins Avenue, Miami Beach - 305 865 6500
★ **Biltmore Hotel**, 1200 Anastasia Avenue - 305 445 1926
★ **Delano Hotel - An Ian Schrager Hotel,** 1685 Collins Avenue, Miami Beach - 305 672 2000
★ **Doral Resort & Country Club**, 4400 Northwest 87th Avenue - 305 592 2000
★ **Hilton Grand Vacations Club**, 1424 Ocean Drive, Miami Beach - 305 604 8225
★ **Hotel Inter-Continental Miami**, 100 Chopin Plaza - 305 577 1000
★ **Hyatt Regency Hotel**, 400 SE 2nd Avenue - 305 358 1234
★ **Loews Miami Beach Hotel**, 1601 Collins Avenue, Miami Beach - 305 604 1601
★ **Sheraton Bal Harbour Beach Resort**, 9701 Collins Avenue, Bal Harbour - 305 865 7511
★ **Sonesta Beach Resort**, 350 Ocean Drive, Key Biscayne - 305 361 2021
★ **Ritz Plaza Hotel Restaurant**, 1701 Collins Avenue, Miami Beach - 305 674 7661

## Office work

★ **Adecco Employment Services**, 11160 Southwest 88th Street - 305 595 4898, info@adeccona.com, www.USAdecco.com
★ **Dixie Staffing Services**, 180 Northwest 183rd Street - 305 770 0077
★ **HT Staffing Services**, 1111 Brickell Avenue, 11th Floor - 305 415 6100, info@htstaffing.net
★ **Kelly Services**, 8603 South Dixie Highway - 305 662 2388
★ **Office Mates 5**, 815 Northwest 57th Avenue - 305 264 4212
★ **Randstad**, 15100 NW 67th Avenue, Miami Lakes - 305 556 9060
★ **Snelling Personnel Services**, 8685 NW 53rd Terrace Suite 103 - 305 591 8835
★ **Southbeach Star Temps**, 12705 Griffing Boulevard, North Miami - 305 865 8500, southbeachstartemps@msn.com
★ **Westaff**, 419 West 49th Street, Hialeah - 305 362 2000

## Language school work

★ **Dynamic English**, 1421 NW 89th Street - 305 597 4064

## Communications

### Internet cafés

★ **Coconut Grove Internet Café**, 2977 McFarlane Road - 305 446 6565
★ **Cyberspace International Café**, 125 SE 2nd Avenue - 305 350 9997

### Libraries

★ **Main Library of Miami**, 101 W Flagler Street - 305 375 2665
★ **Miami Beach Library**, 2100 Collins Avenue - 305 535 4219
★ **Miami Springs Branch**, 401 Westward Drive - 305 884 2575

## Emergencies

**Palm Springs General Hospital**
▤ 1475 W 49th Street
☎ 305 558 2500

**Health South Doctors Hospital (Emergency Room)**
▤ 5000 University Drive, Coral Gables
☎ 305 666 2111

**British Consulate**
▤ Brickell Bay Office Tower, 1001 Brickell Bay Drive, Suite 2800
☎ 305 374 1522

**The North Miami Police Department**
▤ 16901 NE 19th Avenue
☎ 305 949 5500

# new orleans

## Why New Orleans?

Lying on the banks of the Mississippi, New Orleans is an amazing mix of cultures - African, French and Spanish influences combine to produce fantastically tasty food, great music and, of course, Mardis Gras. If you get tired of wandering around and looking at the old French and Spanish architecture, or trying to shop for a daft outfit for the Carnival, there are more than enough great bars, music venues and restaurants for you to overindulge and relax in.

## Some New Orleans facts...

★ New Orleans is one of America's most prominent seaports and is home to nearly 500,000 residents.
★ It's sometimes called the 'Crescent City' because it follows a bend in the river - it covers more than 350 square miles.
★ New Orleans was established in 1718 by Jean Baptiste le Moyne.

## Top things to do in New Orleans

★ Mardi Gras - for revelry, romance, madness and music. It's when the gaudy and the gorgeous all come together for one gigantic party. Just watch and learn!
★ Have a dark roasted coffee and chicory or a white and chocolate milk at the Café du Monde (813 Decatur Street - 504 581 2914), a traditional coffee shop since 1862.
★ New Orleans is big on cemeteries - in fact there are over 40. And because the graves filled with water as soon as they were dug, New Orleans decided to bury their dead above ground. One of the most popular is St Louis Cemetery No 1 where the famous tomb of voodoo queen Marie Laveau is. (Note: you should **never** visit a cemetery on your own.)
★ And if you don't know who Marie Laveau is, you might want to find out more at New Orleans Voodoo (724 Dumaine Street - 504 523 7685)
★ Catch some live music at Tipitina's Uptown (501 Napoleon Avenue - 504 895 8477). Formerly the 501 Club, Tipitina's has earned the reputation as the heart and soul of the New Orleans music community. Harry Connick Jr was just one of many who began his career here.

**The New Orleans Welcome Center**

🖃 529 St Ann Street
☎ 504 566 5031

## Getting there

Louis Armstrong Airport is actually quite small. Only around 15 airlines use the airport and so there aren't many options for getting to the city centre. Jefferson Transit does run an airport bus which is only $1.50 and takes around 15 to 20 minutes.

Trains arrive at Union Station - 1001 Loyla Avenue - and the Greyhound bus terminal is in the same building.

## Getting around

The best way to get around New Orleans is to walk (although be careful where you go outside the French Quarter) - some of the streets are so narrow that buses or cars aren't an option. If you get tired, hop on one of the streetcars - a one-way ticket is $1.50 and one-day visitors' tour pass is only $5.

## Accommodation

### Hostels

★ **HI-New Orleans - Marquette House**, 2249 Carondelet Street - 504 523 3014

★ **India House International Hostel**, 124 South Lopez Street - 504 8211904, info@indiahousehostel.com, www.indiahousehostel.com

★ **Longpré Guest House Hostel**, 1726 Prytania Street - 504 4540 1726

★ **YMCA International Hotel**, 920 Saint Charles Avenue - 504 558 9622

### Camping

★ **Cajun Camping**, 7531 Chef Menteur Highway - 504 242 9039

★ **Mardi Gras Campground**, 6050 Chef Menteur Highway - 504 243 0085

★ **Parc D'Orleans**, 7676 Chef Menteur Highway - 504 241 3164

★ **Riverboat Travel Park**, 6232 Chef Menteur Highway - 800 726 0985

south & florida

# new orleans

## Work

There's a mind-boggling array of bars and restaurants in The Big Easy, so any catering or waiting skills you have will always come in handy. We've listed some of the best here, along with hotels and office temping agencies which might be well worth approaching.

## Bar work

★ **The Balcony Bar**, 3201 Magazine Street - 504 895 1600
★ **The Bulldog**, 3236 Magazine Street - 504 891 1516
★ **Carrollton Station**, 8140 Willow Street - 504 865 9190
★ **Columbia Street Tap Room**, 434 N Columbia Street, Covington - 504 898 0899
★ **Cooter Brown's**, 509 S Carrollton - 504 866 9104
★ **The Crown & Anchor**, 200 Pelican Avenue - 504 227 1007
★ **The Kerry Irish Pub,** 331 Decatur Street - 504 527 5954
★ **Lager's International Ale House**, 3501 Veterans Boulevard, Metairie - 504 887 9923
★ **O'Flaherty's Irish Channel Pub**, 514 Toulouse Street - 504 529 1317
★ **The Rivershack Tavern**, 3449 River Road, Jefferson - 504 835 6933
★ **Ryan's Irish Pub**, 241 Decatur Street - 504 523 3500

## Hotel work

★ **Bourbon Orleans Ramada,** 717 Orleans Avenue - 504 523 2222
★ **Hilton Garden Inn New Orleans Downtown**, 1001 S Peters Street - 504 525 0044
★ **Hilton New Orleans Riverside**, 2 Poydras Street - 504 561 0500
★ **Hotel Inter Continental**, 444 St Charles Avenue - 504 525 5566
★ **Hotel Monteleone**, 214 Royal Street - 866 647 4674
★ **Hyatt Regency New Orleans**, 500 Poydras Plaza - 504 561 1234
★ **Marriott New Orleans**, 555 Canal Street - 504 581 1000

# new orleans

## Hotel work

★ **Omni Royal Crescent Hotel**, 535 Gravier Street - 504 527 0006

★ **Omni Royal Orleans Hotel**, 621 Saint Louis Street - 504 529 5333

★ **Radisson Hotel-New Orleans**, 1500 Canal Street - 504 522 4500

★ **Ritz-Carlton New Orleans**, 921 Canal Street - 504 524 1331

★ **Royal Sonesta Hotel**, 300 Bourbon Street - 504 586 0300

★ **Sheraton New Orleans**, 500 Canal Street - 504 525 2500

★ **Soniat House Hotel**, 1133 Chartres Street - 504 522 0570

★ **W Hotels New Orleans** - W New Orleans, 333 Poydras Street - 504 525 9444

## Office work

★ **Accountemps**, 2574 Place Street Charles - 504 527 0760

★ **Adecco Employment Services**, 1555 Poydras Street - 504 581 9401, info@adeccona.com, www.USAdecco.com

★ **Corporate Personnel Services & Temps**, 15140 Intracoastal Drive - 504 254 9252

★ **Exclusive Temporaries**, 1515 Poydras Street - 504 522 3180

★ **Kelly Services**, 1515 Poydras Street - 504 529 1451

★ **Manpower**, 650 Poydras Street - 504 523 6381

★ **Preferred Temporary Services**, 3300 Esplanade Avenue - 504 835 8085

★ **Professional Temporaries**, 1515 Poydras Street - 504 522 5665

★ **Professional Temp**, 2200 General Meyer Avenue - 504 366 5665

★ **Snelling Personnel Services**, 203 Carondelet Street Suite 530 - 504 529 5781, juliek@snellingneworleans.com

★ **Task Force Temporary Service**, 2929 Tulane Avenue - 504 821 0772

★ **Temps Today**, PO Box 231006 - 504 712 1133

★ **Temps Today Staffing,** 4305 Canal Street - 504 482 4455

★ **Worknet Temporary Employment Services**, 901 Convention Center Boulevard - 504 561 5777

★ **Worktec Temporaries**, 671 Whitney Avenue - 504 368 6952

**south & florida**

south & florida

# new orleans

## Communications

### Internet cafés

★ **The Cyber Bar & Café@The Cac**, 900 Camp Street - 504 523 0990

### Libraries

★ **New Orleans Main Public Library**, 219 Loyola Avenue - 504 529 73 23
★ **Rosa Keller Branch**, 4300 S Broad Street - 504 596 2675
★ **Norman Mayer Branch**, 2098 Foy Street - 504 596 2644
★ **Milton H Latter Memorial Library**, 5120 St Charles Avenue - 504 596 2625

**Times-Picayune Newspaper**
🕸 www.nola.com

## Emergencies

**Charity Hospital**
✉ 1532 Tulane Avenue
☎ 504 568 2311

**New Orleans Police Department**
✉ 1300 Perdido Street
☎ 504 565 7793

## Why Raleigh?

Raleigh is a 'charming' Southern town. It's one of the towns that make up the three points of the 'Research Triangle'. The area (you've guessed it) is a centre for medical and scientific research and many of the leading companies in these fields have a presence here. It's part of a statewide movement towards academic and commercial research, development and innovation.

## Some Raleigh facts...

★    Raleigh was the first American city to have a public art gallery.
★    Pepsi was invented in the state in 1898.

## Top things to do in Raleigh...

★    If you're feeling particularly skint, you can easily spend an afternoon at the Harris Visitors' Center - it may sound just like any old visitor centre but it's actually Carolina Power and Light's nuclear plant with a computer-operated control room simulator. Just be careful what you touch!!

★    Be a museum buff at North Carolina Museum of Art (2110 Blue Ridge Road - 919 839 6262) - a mere 5,000 years' worth of collections from ancient Egyptian artifacts to some contemporary art. They also have concerts, films and entertainment in the grounds in the summer so take your butties and enjoy!

★    OK, everywhere has a farmers' market but the State Farmers' Market in Raleigh seriously takes some beating. It's open every day for everyone - whether you're a serious foodie or just wanting a nosey. It all looks lovely and you'll definitely be tempted.

★    If you've ever had a burning desire to go to a solar demonstration house (c'mon, we know everyone has) then you'll have the good fortune of being able to pop into the North Carolina Solar Center. Don't go on a Saturday though (closed).

★    If you're cited out then chill out at Lake Wheeler Park - you can fish, row, sail, canoe or just watch everyone else doing the hard work and take a well-earned snooze. You can't swim here though - sorry!

**Raleigh Convention & Visitors Bureau**

1 Hannover Square, 421 Fayetteville Street Mall, Suite 1505
800 849 8499
www.raleighcvb.org

south & florida

# raleigh

## Getting there

There is an international airport at Raleigh with shuttle buses running every half an hour - the journey takes about 25 minutes. Visit the TTA website for more information...

☎     919 544 9999
🕸     www.ridetta.org

The Amtrak train station is in downtown Raleigh and it takes about 10 minutes to walk from the station to the city centre. For more info on routes and fares visit Amtrak or Raleigh train station websites...

🕸     www.amtrak.com
🕸     www.bytrain.org

If you prefer travelling by bus there's a Greyhound bus station. For more info call Raleigh bus station or visit the Greyhound website...

☎     301 555 5555
🕸     www.greyhound.com

## Getting around

The best way to get around in Raleigh is to use the Capital Area Transit (CAT) bus system. You can buy a single ticket ($0.75), a 11 ride punch card ($7.50) or a monthly pass ($30.00).

You can buy the passes from the following places...
★     Moore Square station information booth
★     North Carolina State University, administration building
★     All Raleigh Harris Teeter grocery stores
★     Lichford Village Shopping Center, 8320 Lichford Road
★     Townridge Shopping Center, 6544 Glenwood Avenue

## Accommodation

### Camping

★ **Jordan Lake State Recreation Area**, 280 State Park Road - 919 828 9665
★ **William B Umstead State Park**, 8801 Glenwood Avenue - 919 571 4170

### Work

If medical or scientific research is your field, then Raleigh is one of the best places in the US to come and try and get work experience or temporary work. Here's a quick list of a few of the major companies and companies who are based in the 'Research Triangle'...

★ **American Association of Textile Chemists & Colorists**
★ **Bayer Corporation**
★ **GlaxoSmithKline**
★ **Lockheed Martin**
★ **North Carolina Biotechnology Center**
★ **Sony Ericsson Mobile Communications**

Find more at...

 www.rtp.org/owners/otindustry.html

### Bar work

★ **Aura**, 407 Glenwood Avenue - 919 831 1111
★ **The Cellar**, Corner of Dawson & Cabarrus Street - 919 836 9966
★ **Cheers To You**, 5111 Western Boulevard - 919 854 0770
★ **Churchill**, 1622 Glenwood Avenue - 919 831 1525
★ **Club Oxygen**, 412 W Davie Street - 919 812 3188
★ **Club Raleigh**, 218 W Cabarrus Street -919 836 9966
★ **Expressions,** 110 Hargett Street - 919 835 0565
★ **Eclipse Sports Bar**, 240 Paula Street - 919 829 0120
★ **Faces**, 3210 South Wilmington Street - 919 662 9378
★ **Five Café**, 2526 Hillsborough Street - 919 821 4419
★ **Flex**, 2 S West Street - 919 832 8855

# raleigh - work

★ **The Fox & Hound**, Macgregor Shopping Centre -
919 380 0080
★ **Greenshield Brewery and Pub**, 214 E Martin Street -
919 829 0214
★ **King's**, 424 S McDowell Street - 919 891 1005
★ **Legends**, 330 W Hargett Street - 919 831 8888
★ **Loafers Beach Club**, 1625 Capital Boulevard - 919 754 9490
★ **The Office**, 310 S West Street - 919 824 9999
★ **Pericos Bar**, 2414 Paula Street - 919 856 1644
★ **Rum Runners**, 208 E Martin Street - 919 755 6436
★ **Tir Na Nog**, 218 S Blount Street City Market - 919 833 7795

## Hotel work

★ **Best Western**, 3618 New Bern Avenue - 919 231 1099
★ **Cameron Park Inn,** 211 Groveland Avenue - 919 858 2171
★ **Carolina Inn**, 211 Pittsborg Street - 919 929 4000
★ **Crabtree Summit Hotel**, 3908 Arrow Road - 919 782 6868
★ **Embassy Suites**, 4700 Creedmoor Road - 919 881 0000
★ **Extended Stay America**, 3105 Tower Boulevard -
919 489 8444
★ **Fearrington Country Inn**, 2000 Fearrington Village -
919 542 4000
★ **Governors Club**, 1100 Governors Drive - 866 741 1242
★ **Holyday Inn Brownstone**, 1707 Hillsborough Street -
919 828 0811
★ **Holyday Inn Cary**, 5630 Dillard Drive - 919 851 1220
★ **Homewood Suites Hotel - Crabtree Valley**, 5400 Homewood
Banks Drive - 919 785 1131
★ **Jameson Inn**, 2614 S Horner Boulevard - 919 708 7400
★ **Mariott Crabtree Valley**, 4500 Marriot Drive - 919 781 7000
★ **North Raleigh Hilton**, 3415 Wake Forest Road - 919 872 2323
★ **Radisson Plaza Hotel Raleigh**, 420 Fayetteville -
919 832 7055
★ **Sheraton Capital Centre**, 421 S Salisbury - 919 834 9900
★ **Sienna Hotel**, 1505 E Franklin Street - 919 929 4000

## Office work

★ **Apex System**, 4000 West Chase Boulevard Suite 450 - 919 836 1234
★ **AAC Staffing**, 312 W Mill Brook Road Suite 129 - 919 844 2900
★ **Elinvar**, 1804 Hillsborough Street - 919 878 4454
★ **Manpower**, 6500 Falls of the Neuse Suite 130 - 919 876 4022
★ **One Source**, 2841 Plaza Place Suite 110 - 919 834 3331
★ **Sai People Solutions** - 919 755 3800
★ **Todays Staffing**, 4601 Six Forks Road Suite 100 - 919 571 7410
★ **Unicorn Staffing**, 8009 Creedmoor Road - 919 844 1960

**south & florida**

## Communications

### Internet café
★ **Cup a Joe**, 3100 Hillsbrough Street - 919 828 9665

### Public libraries
★ **Green Road Community Library**, 4101 Green Road - 919 790 3200
★ **North Regional Library**, 200 Horizon Drive - 919 870 4000
★ **West Popular Lending Library**, 5800 Duraleigh Road - 919 881 1344

## Emergencies

**Raleigh Community Hospital**
⊟ 3400 Wake Forest Road
☎ 919 954 3492

**Raleigh General Hospital**
⊟ 1710 Harper Road
☎ 304 256 4100

**Police**
⊟ 110 South McDowell Street
☎ 919 890 3183

Stretched out over 1,058 miles (1,702 km) along the West Coast of the USA, the cities of Seattle, Portland, San Francisco, Los Angeles and San Diego are vastly different in culture, people and lifestyle. Think of Seattle and think of trendy cafes; with San Diego it's the beaches. These cities are a great example of the variety of different experiences and ways of life that the USA has to offer.

image courtesy of San Francisco Convention & Visitors Bureau

# los angeles

## Why Los Angeles?

Unless you're looking for a leading role in the next Hollywood blockbuster, there are plenty of opportunities for temporary work in LA. As long as you're not intimidated by it all, you can find your niche here. It takes time to get your head around the geography of the place - the 'City of Angels' is an interesting mix of communities ranging from ritzy Beverly Hills to the not so ritzy South Central area. LA has had bad times and bad press but it is a vibrant and endlessly fascinating city.

## Some Los Angeles facts...
★ The Hollywood sign actually said 'Hollywoodland' until 1945.
★ The 'land' part of the sign slid down the hillside in 1949 and was never replaced.
★ Over 9 million people live in LA County.

## Top things to do in Los Angeles
★ Thanks to John Paul Getty, the Getty Center is home to some impressive permanent art collections and exhibits. Go there and you'll gain much museum-visiting kudos.
★ Visit Mann's Chinese Theater - one of the most famous theatres in the world. It's what Hollywood is all about - grand movie premieres and the legendary 'Forecourt of the Stars'. So join the throngs to one of the most visited attractions in Los Angeles.
★ Go on, you know you have to do it... Put on your best cheesy grin and have your photo taken by the Hollywood sign. It's one to show the grandkids.
★ Go to Santa Monica beach and pretend you're in Baywatch. You could sunbathe but it's more likely that you'll be people-watching. Or you can be wholesome and go for a bike ride (the South Bay Bicycle Trail), surfing or play volleyball. Or you can people-watch some more.
★ Alternatively you can go to Manhattan Beach - it has all the same stuff as Santa Monica beach but it's posher!

## Los Angeles Convention & Visitors Bureau
✉ 685 S Figueroa Street
☎ 213 689 8822
⌂ www.lacvb.com

north west & california

# los angeles

## Getting there

Getting to and from Los Angeles International Airport is easy, which is a good job because it's one of the busiest airports in the world. The Fly Away Bus is reliable and fast. The first bus sets off at 5.30am, the last one departs at midnight and it takes about 30 minutes.

There's also the light rail which makes the journey into town much more comfortable and even faster. Just follow the railway sign after going claiming your bags and you will be in LA in a matter of minutes.

If you are arriving by train to Los Angles, Union Railway Station is on 800 N Alameda Street.

The Greyhound bus terminal is on the east side of the city, on 1716 E 7th Street. For buses or train timetables, go online...

     www.greyhound.com

     www.amtrak.com

## Getting around

Getting around Los Angeles can be a tricky business - public transport is famed for being slow. Big Blue Bus has services on the west of LA and Culver City Bus runs to Culver City and half of west LA. Although the service might be bit slow, it's cheap with single tickets at only $1.00!

If you don't like buses, you've still got the option of the LA Metro which is easy to use. A single ticket on the subway is only $1.35, a weekly pass is $11.00 and a monthly one is $42.00.

## Hostels

★ **Backpackers Paradise**, 4200 West Century Boulevard - 310 672 3090

★ **Cadillac Hotel**, 401 Ocean Front Walk, Venice - 310 399 8876

★ **Central Hotel n Hostel**, 1331-1333 East 7th Street - 213 623 0905

★ **Colonial Inn Hostel**, 421 8th Street Huntington Beach - 714 536 3315, SurfCityHostel@yahoo.com, www.SurfCityHostel.com

★ **Gershwin Hollywood Hotel,** 5533 Hollywood Boulevard, Hollywood - 323 464 1131

★ **Greenleaf Hotel & Hostel**, 63 Lime Avenue, Long Beach - 562 436 5219

★ **HI-Los Angeles - Fullerton**, 1700 North Harbor Boulevard, Fullerton - 714 738 3721

★ **HI-Los Angeles - San Pedro**, 3601 S.Gaffey Street,#613, San Pedro - 310 831 8109

★ **HI-Los Angeles - Santa Monica**, 1436 Second Street, Santa Monica - 310 393 9913

★ **Hollywood International Hostel**, 6820 Hollywood Boulevard, Hollywood - 323 463 0797

★ **Hollywood International Hostel & Hotel**, 1921 North Highland Avenue, Hollywood - 323 876 6544

★ **Hollywood Orange Drive Manor**, 1764 North Orange Drive, Hollywood - 323 850 0350, info@orangedrivehostel.com, www.orangedrivehostel.com

★ **Los Angeles Surf City Hostel**, 26 Pier Avenue, Hermosa Beach - 310 798 2323

★ **Orbit Hotel & Hostel**, 7950 Melrose Avenue, West Hollywood - 323 655 1510, fazilolo@hotmail.com, www.orbithotel.com

★ **Student Inn International Hostel**, 7038 1/2 Hollywood Boulevard, Hollywood - 323 469 6781

★ **USA Hostels - Hollywood**, 1624 Schrader Boulevard, Hollywood - 800 524 6783, hollywood@usahostels.com, www.usahostels.com

★ **Venice Beach Hostel**, 714 Washington Boulevard, Venice Beach - 800 390 2632, info@venicebeahhostel.com, www.venicebeachhostel.com

★ **Venice Beach Hostel & Hotel**, 1515 Pacific Avenue, Venice - 310 452 3052

north west & california

# los angeles

## Work

All the out of work actors and budding Hollywood stars have to work somewhere to pay the rent. The bars, clubs, restaurants and hotels of LA are always looking to take on temporary staff. Here's some of the best places to start looking for work...

## Bar & restaurant work

★ **The Abbey**, 306 Main Street, Seal Beach - 562 799 4246
★ **Barney's Beanery**, 8447 Santa Monica Boulevard - 323 654 2287
★ **BJ's Pizza, Grill & Brewery**, 939 Broxton Avenue - 310 209 7475
★ **Brewski's Brewpub**, 73 Pier Avenue, Hermosa Beach - 310 318 2666
★ **Dockside Brewing #1**, 6272-A East Pacific Coast Highway, Long Beach - 562 431 8211
★ **Dublin's Irish Whiskey Pub**, 8240 W Sunset Boulevard, West Hollywood - 323 656 0100
★ **Frog & Peach Pub**, 728 Higuera Street, San Luis Obispo - 805 595 3764
★ **The Harp Inn**, 130 E 17th Street, Costa Mesa - 714 548 8428
★ **Heroes**, 305 N Harbor Boulevard, Suite 128, Fullerton - 714 738 4356
★ **John Bull English Pub**, 958 S Fair Oaks, Pasadena - 626 441 4353
★ **Lucky Baldwin's**, 17 S Raymond, Pasadena - 626 795 0652
★ **Maggie's Pub**, 11900 Telegraph Road, Santa Fe Springs - 562 944 5399
★ **The Olde Ship Inn**, 709 N Harbor Boulevard, Fullerton - 714 871 7447
★ **Otto's Grill & Beer Bar**, 135 N Grand Avenue - 213 972 7322
★ **Shamrock Bar & Grill**, 2633 W Coast Highway, Newport Beach - 714 631 5633
★ **Stuffed Sandwich**, 413 W Las Tunas Drive, San Gabriel - 626 576 9554
★ **Weber's Place**, 19321 Vanowen Street, Reseda - 818 345 9800
★ **The Yard House**, Shoreline Village, 401 Shoreline Drive, Long Beach - 562 628 0455

# los angeles

## Hotel work

★ **Hollywood Roosevelt Hotel**, 7000 Hollywood Boulevard - 323 466 7000

★ **Le Meridien at Beverly Hills**, 465 South La Cienega Boulevard - 310 247 0400 or 800 645 5687

★ **Le Montrose**, 900 Hammond Street, West Hollywood - 310 855 1115 or 800 776 0666

★ **Sheraton**, 6101 West Century Boulevard - 310 642 1111 or 800 325 3535

★ **Standard Hotel - Downtown-LA**, 550 South Flower Street - 213 892 8080

★ **Standard Hotel - Hollywood**, 8300 West Sunset Boulevard, West Hollywood - 323 650 9090

★ **W Los Angeles - Westwood**, 930 Hilgard Avenue - 310 208 8765

★ **Westin Bonaventure Hotel,** 404 S Figueroa Street - 213 624 1000

## Office work

★ **Accountemps**, 10877 Wilshire Boulevard - 310 209 6800

★ **Adecco**, 11901 Santa Monica Boulevard - 310 209 0663, info@adeccona.com, www.USAdecco.com

★ **Allstaff Temporary Services**, 1512 South Curson Avenue - 323 933 0666

★ **Dee-Mar Temporary Services**, PO Box 45558 - 323 567 9633

★ **Interim Personnel**, 11500 West Olympic Boulevard - 310 477 2999

★ **It's Only Temporary**, 9000 West Sunset Boulevard - 310 777 5443

★ **K & M Temporary Employment Services**, 7822 Santa Monica Boulevard - 323 650 4728

★ **London Temporary Services**, 12424 Wilshire Boulevard - 310 826 3828

★ **Manpower**, 355 South Grand Avenue - 213 745 6500

★ **Personnel Plus** - 818 368 8218, jobs@cme4job.com, www.cme4job.com

★ **Randstad**, 2237 Corinth Avenue - 310 575 9205

★ **Workload Temporary Services**, 315 West 9th Street - 213 489 4482

**north west & california**

# los angeles

**north west & california**

## Language school work

★ **California Language School**, 2975 Wilshire Boulevard - 213 387 8437

★ **English Academy**, 855 Vermont Avenue - 323 663 4958

★ **English Language Center**, 10850 Wilshire Boulevard - 310 470 3019

★ **Wilshire Language School**, 698 S Vermont Avenue - 213 388 5558

## Communications

### Internet cafés

★ **C & C Internet Café**, 7070 W Sunset Boulevard - 323 462 8100

★ **Café Internet**, 4906 Melrose Avenue - 323 462 8782

★ **Café Mac**, 7561 W Sunset Boulevard - 323 466 5600

★ **Plaza Café**, 1818 E 1st Street - 323 268 5787

★ **Techknolotech**, 3300 Overland Avenue- 310 828 8586

★ **Zen Internet Café**, 7264 Melrose Avenue - 323 938 6521

### Libraries

★ **Central Library**, 630 W 5th Street - 213 228 7000

★ **Ascot Branch**, 256 W 70th Street - 323 759 4817

★ **Chinatown Branch**, 639 N Hill Street - 213 620 0925

## Emergencies

**British Consulate-General**

≡ 11766 Wilshire Boulevard, Suite 1200

☎ 310 481 0031

**USC University Hospital**

≡ 1500 San Pablo Street

☎ 323 422 8500

**Los Angeles Police**

≡ 251 E 6th Street

☎ 213 485 3284

# portland

## Why Portland?

Portland is an outstandingly beautiful city to live and work in, with its stunning views of the mountains and its position on the Williamette River. It's a great city to live in all year round and business is booming in this former logging town. The industries are now a bit more high-tech and the city is being redeveloped at a great pace, but it's still a great place to be. It has easy access to great skiing and hiking areas so it's a particularly cool city to live in if you're into the great outdoors.

## Some Portland facts...

★ Portland is known as the city of roses.
★ The state fish is the Chinnook salmon.
★ The state flag has got a beaver on it.

## Top things to do in Portland...

★ If books are your thing then Powell's Book Store is your place. Would you believe that it covers an entire city block? So you won't be surprised to know it's the largest new and used bookstore in the world. It's quite something.

★ Come on, be honest, don't you have just a bit of a soft spot for roses? We guarantee the Portland Rose Garden will take your breath away so make sure you fit the world famous gardens in on your whistle stop tour of the US.

★ And while we're on the topic of gardens, Portland's Chinese Gardens must be visited. It's the largest garden of its kind outside China. A great place to chill out.

★ Situated high in the West Hills, the Pittock Mansion is well worth a trip. It was built by Henry Pittock, one of Portland's most prominent pioneers, and is a big part of the city's history.

★ If you're feeling flush, see what's on at the Rose Quarter (the answer seems to be everything). Rock concerts, NBA games, figure skating, the circus - anything big in town happens at Portland's newly built stadium.

★ Peruse the lovely, lovely arty things at the Portland Saturday Market - with over 300 artisans there are lots of opportunities to spend...

## Portland Convention & Visitors Bureau

245 Commercial Street
207 772 5800
www.visitportland.com

# portland

## Getting there

### By air

Portland has a busy international airport and major airlines like American Airlines and Continental have regular flights there. From the airport there is a quick train connection to the city centre. A one way trip on the Max Red Line train is only $1.55 and it takes 38 minutes!

If you are arriving by rail, the station is on the edge of downtown on NW 6th Avenue. It's worth knowing that the line closely follows the Rocky Mountains so the trains provide extra space for bikes, skies and snowboards.

The Greyhound bus station is close to the railway station on 550 NW 6th Avenue. For more info about timetables and fares...

     www.greyhound.com

## Getting around

Most of Portland's public transport is run by TriMet. The trams and buses are frequent, reliable and easy to use. A single fare is $1.55 and a ten ticket pass costs $14.50. If you're planning to stay in Portland longer, you can buy a monthly pass for $56. You can buy the passes from Safeway's, Fred Meyer, Albertson's and from TriMet's customer service in Pioneer Square. For more info...

     www.trimet.org

# Accommodation

## Hostels

★ **HI-Portland - Hawthorne District**, 3031 SE Hawthorne Boulevard - 503 236 3380, hip@portlandhostel.org, www.portlandhostel.org
★ **HI-Portland - Northwest**, 1818 NW Glisan Street - 503 241 2783, hinwp@teleport.com, www.2oregonhostels.com

## Camping

★ **Eagle Creek Campground**, East 1-84 Exit 41 - 541 386 2333
★ **Oregon State Park**, 1-84 Exit 35 Columbia Gorge - 800 551 6949

## Work

Portland and the state of Oregon are famous for logging and mining but if you don't fancy wearing a lumberjack shirt then there are plenty of other options. The city's industries are now more based on silicon chips than wood chips, and there many fresh new technology companies, as well as the usual bar and waiting jobs.

## Bar & restaurant work

★ **The Black Cat Pub**, 8230 SE 13th Avenue - 503 235 3571
★ **Bookies Sports Bar**, 736 North Lombard Street - 503 286 7520
★ **BridgePort Ale House**, 3632 SE Hawthorne Boulevard - 503 233 6540
★ **Carmichael's Public & Grill**, 12740 Southwest Pacific Highway - 503 624 0243
★ **Coach's Bar & Grill**, 10162 SW Park Way - 503 203 8250 8
★ **Etcetera Tavern**, 3276 NE Killingsworth Street - 503 282 2411
★ **Grandstand Pub & Grill**, 11525 Southwest Durham Road, Tigard - 503 598 9220
★ **Jimmy's Sports Bar**, 3017 Southwest Multnomah Boulevard - 503 293 2100

# portland

★ **Magic Gardens Restaurant & Lounge**, 217 NW 4th Avenue -
503 224 8472
★ **McCall's Waterfront Cafe**, 1020 SW Front Avenue -
503 248 9710
★ **The Mockcrest Tavern**, 3435 North Lombard Street -
503 283 5014
★ **Scandals Restaurant & Lounge**, 1038 SW Stark Street -
503 227 5887
★ **Wired Sports Bar**, 11340 Northeast Halsey Street -
503 252 4833

## Hotel work

★ **The Benson Hotel**, 309 SW Broadway Street - 503 228 2000
★ **The Governor Hotel**, 611 SW 10th Avenue - 503 224 3400
★ **Hilton Portland,** 921 Southwest 6th Avenue - 503 226 1611
★ **Mallory Hotel**, 729 Southwest 15th Avenue - 503 223 6311
★ **Radisson Hotel Portland**, 1441 NE 2nd Avenue -
503 233 2401
★ **Ramada Inn Rose Quarter**, 10 North Weidler Street -
503 287 9900
★ **Vintage Plaza Hotel**, 422 SW Broadway - 503 228 1212
★ **Westin Portland**, 750 SW Alder Street - 503 294 9000

## Office work

★ **Accountemps**, 222 Southwest Columbia Street - 503 222 9778

★ **Adams Temporaries**, 121 Southwest Morrison Street - 503 224 5870

★ **Adecco Employment Services**, 700 North Hayden Island Drive - 503 283 1355

★ **Brooks Staffing**, 1130 Northeast Alberta Street - 503 284 7930

★ **Contractors Temporary Employment Service**, 2700 Southeast Harrison Street - 503 654 0021

★ **Employers Overload**, 9225 Southwest Hall Boulevard - 503 624 8000, tempinfo@eostaffing.com

★ **Express Personnel Services**, 9055 SW Beaverton Hillsdale Highway - 503 292 1200

★ **Kelly Services**, 700 Northeast Multnomah Street - 503 230 2221

★ **Kennedy Temporary Service**, 220 NW 2nd Avenue Suite 660 - 503 222 3307

★ **Manpower**, 1000 Southwest Broadway - 503 226 6281

★ **Olsten Staffing Services**, 10220 Southwest Greenburg Road - 503 244 5664

★ **Randstad**, 111 SW 5th Avenue - 503 790 9303

★ **Selectemp Corporation**, 9011 Southwest Beaverton Hillsdale - 503 296 9670

★ **Temporary Staffing**, 421 Southwest 6th Avenue - 503 221 0338

## Language schools

★ **American Language Academy**, 5000 N Willamette Boulevard - 503 452 4160, www.ala-usa.com

★ **Columbia Education Center**, 11325 South East Lexington - 503 760 2346

★ **Ecole French School**, 6318 SW Corbett Avenue - 503 452 4160

★ **Pacific International Academy**, 17600 Pacific Highway 43 Marylhurst - 503 699 6310

north west & california

# portland

## Communications

### Internet cafés

★ **Brewchats Cybercafé**, 6660 SW Capitol Highway - info@brewchats.com, www.brewchats.com

★ **Fireside Coffee Lodge**, 1223 SE Powell Boulevard - 503 230 8987

★ **Heaven**, 421 SW 10th Street - 503 243 6152

★ **Internet Arena**, 1016 SW Taylor - 503 224 2718, support@inetarena.com, http://inetarena.com

★ **Millennium Café**, 2633 SE 21st Avenue - 503 235 9945, info@millenium.portland.or.us, http://millenim.portland.or.us

★ **Web21 Internet Café**, 2101 NW Hoyt Street - 503 706 0021, general@web21cafe.com

### Libraries

★ **Clalmas Corner Library**, 11750 SE 82nd Avenue - 503 722 6222

★ **Hoodland Library**, 68236 E Highway 26 Welches - 503 622 3460

★ **Oak Lodge library**, 16201 SE McLouglin Boulevard - 503 655 8543

### Emergencies

★ **Pacific Gateway Hospital,** 1345 SE Harney Street - 503 234 5353

★ **Portland Police Bureau,** 111 SW 2nd Avenue - 503 823 4636

# san diego

## Why San Diego?

Grand old buildings and a beautiful seafront with clean beaches - who wouldn't want to live and work here? Whether you fancy lazing on the beach in the Californian sunshine or relaxing in the city's beautiful Balboa Park, life in San Diego is at a relaxed pace. It's also got plenty of great bars to work in or wind down in after your hard day on the beach. And its proximity to Mexico means its restaurants are something special. Fine weather, good food and a lively cultural scene make San Diego a very good place to hang out for a while.

## Some San Diego facts...

★ San Diego is the oldest city in California.
★ San Diego has 70 miles of beaches.
★ With a population of about 1,110,554 people, San Diego is the second largest city in California.

## Top things to do in San Diego...

★ Get a tan. The city has previously been voted the only area in the United States with perfect weather conditions - it has an average annual temperature of 70°F (20°C).
★ Say hello to the 4000 rare and endangered animals at the famous San Diego Zoo.
★ Wander for hours, in fact days, in Balboa Park. It's bigger than Central Park and offers everything from Shakespeare to live elephants (work that one out!)
★ Do some free museum cruising (you can get into a lot of museums for free on Tuesdays). There's the Museum of Photographic Arts, Mingei International Museum, San Diego Art Institute, The Timken Art Gallery, Spanish Village Art Center, Natural History Museum, San Diego Historical Society, Centro Cultural de la Raza, Aerospace Museum, The Hall of Champions, The Automotive Museum, Fleet Science Center, The Model Railroad Museum and The Museum of Man. Just a few to start you off.
★ If you're after food, fun, culture or entertainment, then look no further than the Gaslamp Quarter - 70 restaurants within walking distance and happy hours galore!
★ Promenade along the Embarcadero, a paved pedestrian path leading to an assortment of all things harbour-related including restaurants, boat tours, fish markets and shops.

# san diego

★ Pop to Mexico for the day. Tijuana is only 17 miles from downtown San Diego and an easy trip on the San Diego Trolley ($2.25 each way). And don't forget your passport!

★ Be wowed at the Museum of Contemporary Art. The setting is great - from the top of the grand stairway, you can look out to a beautiful garden and the Pacific. Most of the artwork at the museum celebrates the work of California artists (700 Prospect Street - 619 454 3541)

**San Diego Convention & Visitors Bureau**

✉ 401 B Street

☎ 619 236 1212

🕸 www.sandiego.org

## Getting there

San Diego Lindbergh Field Airport is just three miles from downtown San Diego with the Coaster Train Link connecting them. If you'd rather take an airport bus just follow the bus sign after the baggage claim. The route 992 runs regularly between the airport and city centre.

San Diego Santa Fe railway station is a beautiful old Spanish colonial style building - a great place to arrive into. The Greyhound bus terminal is downtown on 120 W Broadway.

## Getting around

Buses, trains and trolleys criss-cross the city making getting around very easy. One way on the bus is $1.50.

San Diego is also famous for being a bike-friendly city. The bike routes around and outside the city are fantastic. There are loads of places in the city centre where you can hire a bike. Try...

★ **Bike Rentals San Diego,** 509 5th Avenue - 619 238 2444

And remember that in San Diego you can take your bike on the bus for free!

## Accommodation

### Hostels

★ **HI-San Diego - Point Loma**, 3790 Udall Street -
619 223 4778, www.sandiegohostels.com
★ **HI-San Diego - The Metropolitan**, 521 Market Street -
619 525 1531, www.sandiegohostels.com
★ **International House at the 2nd Floor**, 4502 Cass Street,
Pacific Beach - 858 274 4325
★ **Ocean Beach International Backpackers Hostel**, 4961
Newport Avenue - 800 339 7263, OBIhostel@aol.com,
www.californiahostel.com
★ **USA Hostels - San Diego**, 726 5th Avenue - 800 438 8622,
Sandiego@usahostels.com, www.usahostels.com

## Work

Fantastic restaurants and bars are definitely San Diego's forte - a good place to find temporary work.

## Bar work

★ **BJ's Pizza, Grill & Brewery**, 8873 Villa La Jolla - 619 455 0662
★ **Blarney Stone**, 502 5th Avenue - 619 233 8519
★ **Gaslamp Brewing**, 500 Fourth Avenue - 619 239 9117
★ **Hooley's Irish Pub & Grill**, 2955 Jamacha Road, Suite 21,
Rancho San Diego - 619 670 7468
★ **Newport Avenue Bar & Grill**, 4935 Newport Avenue -
619 222 0168
★ **O'Brien's Pub**, 4646 Convoy Street - 858 715 1745
★ **Oggi's Pizza & Brewing Co**, North County Fair Mall, 200 East
via Ranch Parkway, #201, Escondido - 760 466 1000
★ **Oggi's Pizza & Brewing Co**, 305 Encinitas Boulevard, Encinitas
- 760 944 8170
★ **Princess of Wales**, 1665 India Street - 619 238 1266
★ **Shakespeare's Pub**, 3701 India Street - 619 299 0230
★ **Tom Giblin's Irish Pub**, 640-A Grand Avenue, Carlsbad
★ **The Yard House**, 1023 4th Avenue

**north west & california**

# san diego

## Hotel work

★ **Hacienda Hotel**, Old Town Juan & Harney - 619 298 4707

★ **Hilton Hotel-Mission Valley**, 901 Camino Del Rio South - 619 543 9000

★ **Hilton Hotel-Mission Bay Beach & Tennis RE**, 1775 East Mission Bay Drive - 619 276 4010

★ **Hilton La Jolla Torrey Pine**s - 858 558 1500, www.lajollatorreypines.hilton.com

★ **Hilton San Diego Airport**, 1960 Harbor Island Drive - 619 291 6700

★ **Hilton San Diego Gaslamp Quarter**, 401 K Street - 619 231 4040

★ **Hilton San Diego Resort**, 1775 East Mission Bay Drive - 619 276 4010, www.sandiegoresort.hilton.com

★ **Horton Grand Hotel & Suites**, 311 Island Avenue - 619 544 1886

★ **Hotel Del Coronado**, 1500 Orange Avenue, Coronado - 619 522 8158

★ **Hyatt Regency Islandia**, 1441 Quivira Road - 619 224 1234

★ **Shelter Point Hotel & Marina**, 1551 Shelter Island Drive - 619 221 8000

★ **Sheraton San Diego East Tower**, 1380 Harbor Island Drive - 619 692 2793

★ **US Grant Hotel**, 326 Broadway - 619 232 3121

★ **Westgate Hotel the Reservations**, 1055 2D Avenue - 619 238 1818

★ **Westin Horton Plaza**, 910 Broadway Circle - 619 239 2200

## Office work

★ **Accountemps**, 9820 Willow Creek Road - 858 547 1188
★ **Adecco Employment Services**, 9450 Scranton Road - 858 554 0013, info@adeccona.com, www.USAdecco.com
★ **Appleone Employment Services**, 8590 Rio - 619 542 1310
★ **Eastridge Group the Temporary Staffing**, 2355 Northside Drive - 619 260 2100
★ **Eastridge Temps**, 2355 Northside Drive - 619 260 2040
★ **Express Personnel Services**, 6755 Mira Mesa Boulevard - 858 784 3676, www.expresspersonnel.com
★ **Kelly Services**, 2878 Camino Del Rio South - 619 298 6600
★ **Manpower Temporary Services**, 10875 Rancho Bernardo Road - 858 676 2201
★ **Meridian Temporary Services**, 4320 La Jolla Village Drive - 858 455 7500
★ **Professional Temporary Employment Service**, 1850 5th Avenue - 619 325 2415

## Language school work

★ **American Language Institution**, 5250 Campanile Drive - 619 594 5907
★ **Berlitz Language Center**, 225 Broadway -619 235 8344
★ **College of English Language**, 625 Broadway - 619 234 7466
★ **International Academy - English**, 1727 5th Avenue - 619 232 8768
★ **International House**, 2725 Congress Street - 619 299 2339

north west & california

# san diego

## Communications

### Internet cafés
★ **Internet Corner**, 800 Broadway - 619 702 2233
★ **Lalin Cyber Café**, 3556 University Avenue - 619 521 2836
★ **Mirage Coffee Co**, 1602 Front Street - 619 231 6313

### Libraries
★ **Central Library**, 820 E Streets - 619 236 5800
★ **Balboa Branch**, 4255 MT Abernathy Avenue - 858 573 1390
★ **Linda Vista Branch**, 2160 Ulrich Street - 858 573 1399

**San Diego Union-Tribune Newspaper**
&#x2690; www.uniontrib.com

## Emergencies

**Emergency Department**
✉ 200 W Arbour Drive
☎ 619 543 640

**Mission Bay Hospital**
✉ 3030 Bunker Hill Street
☎ 619 274 7721

**Lifeguard Headquarters**
☎ 619 224 2708 for medical enquiries

**San Diego Police Department**
✉ 7222 Skyline Drive
☎ 619 527 3500

# san francisco

## Why San Francisco?

San Francisco is not only one of the coolest looking cities in the US, with funky old houses clinging to its hills, but it's also home to all things radical and forward thinking. Its history has been shaped by the movements that have grown here - the Beat Generation in the fifties; hippies, student activists and Black Power groups in the sixties; gay rights movement in the seventies. Haight Ashbury may now be a bit of a sixties theme park but San Francisco still has its old magic and dynamism.

## Some San Francisco facts...

★ The Golden Gate Bridge was completed in 1937 after four years and a mere $35 million.

★ The 1.2 mile structure is the second longest single-suspension bridge in the world and contains two cables with enough steel wire (80,000 miles) to go around the equator three times.

★ Alcatraz is Spanish for 'pelican'.

## Top things to do in San Francisco...

★ Take a trip to Alcatraz Island, in the middle of San Francisco Bay, once home of Al Capone and Robert Franklin Stroud (the 'Birdman of Alcatraz').

★ Check out the amazing views of the San Francisco skyline, Alcatraz and the Marin Headlands from the Golden Gate Bridge but be careful - it can often sway 27 feet in high winds!

★ You want weird? Try the Ripley's Believe it Or Not Museum (south side of Jefferson Street - 415 771 6188) for 'oddball, silly, weird and funny attractions' that you can believe (or not!).

★ Visit the Castro, San Francisco's 'Gay Mecca'. The area was responsible for electing San Francisco's first openly gay politician - Harvey Milk. Castro Street is particularly good for books, cappuccino, male dolls and Asian noodles!

★ Take in the 9000 photographs, 3200 architectural drawings and 5500 paintings at the SF MoMA - that's the San Francisco Museum of Modern Art to you and I. But don't go on Wednesdays or you won't see much (it's closed!)

## San Francisco Visitors Information Center

🖃 900 Market Street

☎ 415 391 2000

🏠 www.sfvisitor.org

# san francisco

## Getting there

San Francisco Airport is south of San Francisco. The airport can get quite busy because it handles San Francisco's domestic and international connections to Europe, Latin America and Pacific. But that makes getting to the airport and back easy. There's a direct train service from Millbrae to San Francisco with free buses running between Millbrae station and the airport. The first train goes at 5.00am and the last one leaves Millbrae Station at 11.59pm.

There are also airport buses - SanTrans buses have direct service to city centre.

Amtrak doesn't have a station in the centre of San Francisco. The trains stop at Jack London Square in Oakland but there is a free shuttle connection to San Francisco.

If you are arriving by bus, the Greyhound bus terminal is on 425 Mission Transbay Street.

## Getting around

San Francisco Municipal Railway (MUNI) runs the city's public transport. Buses, trolleybuses and cable cars are easy to use. It's $2 to use and you can buy tickets onboard. A weekly pass is $9. Or if you want to 'do San Francisco' in a day, you can get a city pass ($34) which covers most of the city's sites and public transport - definitely worth considering.

## Accommodation

### Hostels

★ **Adelaide Hostel**, 5 Isadora Duncan Lane - 415 359 1915, info@adelaidehostel.com, www.adelaidehostel.com

★ **California Dreamin'**, 3145-47 Mission Street - 415 552 8452

★ **Globe Hostel**, 10 Hallam Place - 415 431 0540, gspot@globe-hostel.com, www.globe-hostel.com

★ **Globetrotters Inn Hostel**, 225 Ellis Street - 415 346 5786

★ **Green Tortoise Backpackers Guesthouse**, 494 Broadway - 415 834 1000

★ **HI-San Francisco - City Center**, 685 Ellis Street - 415 474 5721

★ **HI-San Francisco - Downtown**, 312 Mason Street - 415 788 5604

★ **HI-San Francisco - Fishermans Wharf**, Fort Mason, Building 240 - 415 771 7277

★ **Home Away International Hostel**, 555 Haight Street - 415 864 4646

★ **International Guest House**, 2976 23rd Street - 415 641 1411

★ **International Student Center**, 1188 Folsom Street - 415 255 8800

★ **Mission Hostel @ El Capitan Hotel**, 2361 Mission Street - 415 695 1597, www.hostelhandbook.com/missionhostel

★ **New Central Hotel & Hostel**, 1412 Market Street - 415 703 9988

★ **Pacific Tradewinds Hostel**, 680 Sacramento Street - 415 433 7970, tradewinds@hostels.com, www.hostels.com/pt/

★ **Pontiac Hotel & Hostel**, 509 Minna Street - 415 863 7775

**north west & california**

# san francisco

## Work

San Francisco is arguably the financial hub of the West Coast, and is home to a lot of the region's big business. There's also plenty of work in many of the city's bars and restaurants. It's a great base if you are trying to find work in the world's leading centre for new technologies, research and development, because it's the nearest big city to the 'Silicon Valley' area.

## Bar work

- ★ **Ben 'n Nicks**, 5612 College Avenue - 510 923 0327
- ★ **Betelnut**, 2030 Union Street - 415 929 8855
- ★ **Brew City**, 1370 Locust Street, Walnut Creek - 510 930 9844
- ★ **Britannia Arms**, 1087 Sunnyvale Road, San Jose - 408 252 7262
- ★ **Cafe du Nord**, 2170 Market - 415 861 5016
- ★ **City Pub**, 2620 Broadway, Redwood City - 650 363 2620
- ★ **Edinburgh Castle**, 950 Geary Street - 415 885 4074
- ★ **Empire Room**, 651 Emerson, Palo Alto - 650 321 3030
- ★ **Ginsberg's Dublin Pub**, 400 Bay - 415 771 3760
- ★ **Hamburger Mary's**, 1582 Folsom - 415 626 1985
- ★ **Ireland's 32**, 3920 Geary - 415 386 6173
- ★ **The Irish Bank**, 10 Mark Lane - 415 788 7152
- ★ **Jacks at the Cannery,** 2801 Leaveanworth - 415 931 6400
- ★ **Mayflower Inn,** 1533 4th Street, San Rafael - 415 456 1011
- ★ **Mission Ale House**, 97 E Santa Clara, San Jose - 408 292 4058
- ★ **O'Kane's Irish Pub**, 97 Prescott, Monterey - 408 375 7564
- ★ **Plough & Stars**, 116 Clement - 415 751 1122
- ★ **Poet & Patriot**, 320 E Cedar Street - 408 426 8620
- ★ **Prince Of Wales**, 106 E 25th Avenue, San Mateo - 650 574 9723
- ★ **Raleighs**, 2438 Telegraph, Berkeley - 510 848 8652
- ★ **Rat & Raven**, 4054 24th Street - 415 285 0674
- ★ **The Royal Exchange,** 301 Sacramento - 415 956 1710
- ★ **Starry Plough**, 3001 Shattuck, Oakland - 510 841 2082
- ★ **Toronado**, 547 Haight Street - 415 863 2276
- ★ **Trials Pub**, 265 North First Street, San Jose - 408 947 0497
- ★ **Vintage Cellar Bistro**, 1001 B Street, Hayward - 510 886 8525

## Hotel work

- ★ **Argent Hotel San Francisco**, 50 3D - 415 974 6400, argenthotel@destinationhotels.com
- ★ **Beresford Arms Hotel**, 701 Post Street - 415 673 2600
- ★ **Best Western Americania**, 121 7th Street - 415 626 0200
- ★ **Best Western Tuscan Inn at Fishermans Wharf**, 425 North Point Street - 415 561 1100
- ★ **Cathedral Hill Hotel**, 1101 Van Ness Avenue - 415 776 8200
- ★ **Clarion Hotel Bedford Hotel At Union**, 761 Post Street - 415 673 6040
- ★ **Clift Hotel**, Geary & Taylor - 415 775 4700
- ★ **Grand Hyatt San Francisco**, 345 Stockton Street - 415 398 1234
- ★ **Harbor Court Hotel**, 165 Steuart Street - 415 882 1300
- ★ **Hilton San Francisco & Towers**, 333 Ofarrell Street - 415 771 0720
- ★ **Sheraton at Fishermans Wharf**, 2500 Mason Street - 415 362 5500
- ★ **Westin St Francis**, 335 Powell Street - 415 774 0112

## Office work

- ★ **ABA Staffing**, 690 Market Street - 415 434 4222, info@abastall.com
- ★ **Accountemps**, 50 California Street - 415 434 1900
- ★ **Adecco Employment Services**, 44 Montgomery Street - 415 434 3810, info@adeccona.com, www.USAdecco.com
- ★ **Compuforce**, 140 Geary Street - 415 392 5856
- ★ **Key Resources**, 111 Pine Street - 415 394 8383
- ★ **Manpower**, 50 California Street - 415 781 7171
- ★ **Officeteam**, 50 California Street - 415 434 2429
- ★ **Randstad**, 100 Spear Street - 415 537 9660
- ★ **Remedy Personnel Services**, 595 Market Street - 415 243 8566
- ★ **Student Source**, 870 Market Street - 415 788 7279, student@studentsource.com
- ★ **Tempositions**, 140 Geary Street - 415 392 5856
- ★ **Temptime Temporary Service**, 211 Sutter Street - 415 732 7520

**north west & california**

# san francisco

## Communications

**San Francisco Chronicle - newspaper**
 www.sfgate.com/chronicle/

## Emergencies

**San Francisco General Hospital**
⌑ 1001 Potrero Avenue
☎ 415 206 8000

**Haight Ashbury Free Clinic**
⌑ 558 Clayton Street
☎ 415 487 5632

**British Consulate-General**
⌑ 1 Sansome Street, Suite 850
☎ 415 617 1300

image copyright: San Francisco Convention & Visitors Bureau

## Why Seattle?

Seattle has developed a reputation as a centre for innovation and funky ideas - coffee shops, grunge rock, computers. But not everybody in the city works for Microsoft (at least not all of the time!) and the city has a very lively cultural life. There is a great café scene here and the city's music has been a trendsetter for the rest of the world. Seattle is in the beautiful surroundings of Puget Sound and Lake Washington and is an fresh and invigorating place to live and work. And, of course, you'll never be short of good coffee and getting your computer fixed is a doddle!

## Some Seattle facts...

★ Seattle is the birthplace of Jimi Hendrix.
★ Seattle is the home of Starbucks coffee.
★ The first revolving restaurant was in Seattle.

## Top things to do in Seattle...

★ If you want to feel on top of the world, just pop up to the top of the Space Needle. A mere 52 storeys into the sky with a 360 degree view. On a clear day you can see it all and more.
★ Get wired and amped up the Experience Music Project - a tribute to Jimi Hendrix and the art of rock 'n' roll.
★ Get some fresh fish and food delights at Pike Place Market - some describe it as the soul (sole?) of the city.
★ Say hello to the 48 foot Hammering Man at Seattle Art Museum. Their collection of Native American art is also well worth a look.
★ You could spend hours at Hiram M Chittenden Locks just watching the boats go up. And down. And up.
★ Take advantage of free admission one day a month at Seattle Art Museum, Seattle Asian Art Museum, Wing Luke Asian Museum. It's worth mentioning that the Center for Wooden Boats, Frye Art Museum and Klondike Gold Rush National Park are also free. Bonus.

## Seattle Convention & Visitors Bureau

🖃 1 Convention Place, 701 Pike Street, Suite 800
☎ 206 461 5840
🕸 www.seeseattle.org

north west & california

# seattle

north west & california

## Getting there

Seattle-Tacoma can get quite hectic - the airport is a gateway for people wanting to travel to Canada, Europe or the Pacific.

Shuttles, taxis and public buses run between the airport and the city constantly. The airport bus departs twice an hour and a one way journey costs $8.50. There's also a public bus for $1.25.

Amtrak trains arrive in King St Station on 401 S Jackson Street. Greyhound buses have two stations in Seattle - one on 811 Stewart Street and one at the railway station.

## Getting around

Metro Transit runs the metropolitan area and Seattle Trolley Tours looks after the downtown area. The buses are easy to use and relatively cheap. A one way ticket downtown is around $1.25.

The best way to see Seattle is by boat. There are ferries from Seattle port to nearby islands and to Canada. For info about routes and fares, visit the Washington State Department of Transport website...

   www.wsdot.wa.gov

## Accommodation

### Hostels

★ **Green Tortoise Backpackers Hostel**, 1525 Second Avenue - 206 340 1222
★ **HI-Seattle**, 84 Union Street - 206 622 5443
★ **HI-Seattle Vashion Ayh Ranch Hostel**, 12119 Southwest Cove Road - 206 463 2592, dirk@vashonhostel.com, www.vashonhostel.

### Camping

★ **Camp Ten Trees**, 111 5 E Pike Street - 206 324 1811

146. usa gap pack

# Work

There's more to Seattle than just computers and coffee and, as a centre for business innovation and entrepreneurial spirit, you'll find that there are plenty of employers in Seattle ready to give you a chance if you can show the right skills and the right attitude.

## Bar work

- ★ **Garage**, 1130 Broadway - 206 322 2296
- ★ **George & Dragon Pub**, 206 North 36th Street - 206 545 6864
- ★ **J & M Cafe & Cardroom**, 201 1st Avenue S - 206 292 0663
- ★ **Jersey's Sports Bar,** 2004 7th Avenue - 206 343 9377
- ★ **Maritime Pacific Brewing Company**, 1514 New Leary Way - 206 782 6181
- ★ **Murphy's Pub**, 1928 North 45th Street - 206 634 2110
- ★ **Parker's Sports Bar & Casino**, 17001 Aurora Avenue North - 206 542 9491
- ★ **Pexos Sports Bar & Grill**, 12725 Lake City Way Northeast - 206 362 2911
- ★ **Rainbow Bar & Grill**, 722 Northeast 45th Street - 206 634 1761
- ★ **Seattle's Historic Triangle Pub**, 553 1st Avenue S - 206 628 0474
- ★ **Tini Bigs Lounge**, 100 Denny Way - 206 284 0931

## Hotel work

- ★ **Hawthorn Inn & Suites**, 2224 8th Avenue - 206 624 6820
- ★ **Hilton Downtown** - 6th & University - 206 624 0500
- ★ **Hotel Monaco,** 1101 4th Avenue - 206 621 1770
- ★ **Ramada Inn Downtown Seattle**, 2200 5th Avenue - 206 441 9785
- ★ **Seattle Marriott**, 3201 South 176th Street - 206 241 2000
- ★ **Seattle Westin**, 1900 5th Avenue - 206 728 1000
- ★ **Sheraton Seattle Hotel & Towers**, 1400 6th Avenue - 206 621 9000
- ★ **Silver Cloud Inns Seattle**, 5036 25th Avenue Northeast - 206 526 5200

**north west & california**

# seattle

## Office work

★   **Adams Temporaries,** 16400 Southcenter Parkway -
     206 575 6266
★   **Adecco Employment Services**, 601 Union Street -
     206 464 1616
★   **AM Temporaries**, The Columbia Centre - 206 447 9200
★   **Express Personnel Services**, 2401 4th Avenue Suite 150 -
     206 443 5627
★   **Hallmark Temps** - 206 587 5327
★   **Kelly Services**, 999 3rd Avenue - 206 382 7171
★   **Manpower - Seattle Downtown**, 1420 5th Avenue -
     206 583 0880
★   **Molly Brown Temps**, 520 Pike Street - 206 628 0598
★   **Pace Staffing Network**, 720 3rd Avenue - 206 623 1050
★   **Skilltemp**, 13985 Interurban Avenue South - 206 835 1368
★   **Spherion - Clerical**, 900 4th Avenue - 206 340 8854
★   **Temporarily Yours**, 720 3rd Avenue - 206 386 5400
★   **TTS United Temp Service**, 9421 16th Avenue Southwest -
     206 768 0892

## Language school work

★   **ALPS Language School**, 216 Broadway Street Suite 202 -
     202 720 6363
★   **Seattle Language Academy**, 126 NW Canal Street -
     206 325 4109
★   **Speakeasy**, 2222 2nd Avenue - 206 728 9770

## Communications

### Internet cafés

★ **Online Coffee Company**, 1111 1st Avenue - 206 381 1911
★ **Online Coffee Company**, 1720 E Olive Way
★ **Seattle Street Coffee**, 456 Geary Avenues - 415 922 4566

### Libraries

★ **Seattle Public Library**, 800 Pike Street - 206 386 4636
★ **Ballard Branch**, 5711 24th Avenue - 206 684 4089
★ **Beacon Hill Branch**, 2519 15th Avenue - 206 684 4711
★ **Columbia Branch**, 4721 Rainier Avenue - 206 615 1329

## Emergencies

**British Consulate**
✉ 900 Fourth Avenue, Suite 3001
☎ 206 622 9255

**Northwest Hospital**
✉ 1550 N 115th Street
☎ 206 364 0500

**Seattle Police Headquarters**
✉ 619 Fifth Avenue
☎ 202 625 5011

It's not all sand and snakes, cactuses and card-sharps in North America's South West - it's an area full of dramatic contrasts, between cultures, ethnic groups and natural and urban environments. From ultra-modern cities like Phoenix to ancient Pueblo Indian communities, the differences are striking. Architecture, ambition and a lot of money come together to make Las Vegas one of the weirdest places on Earth, while the vastness and natural beauty of the Grand Canyon will take your breath away. The South West is an amazingly diverse place to live, work in and explore.

image courtesy of Nevada Commission on Tourism

# las vegas

## Why Las Vegas?

Las Vegas, like New York, is a city that will seem strangely familiar to you from films and television. However nothing can really prepare you for the sensory assault that the city's casinos, bars and restaurants have become. Despite its reputation as a tourist destination, it is also a place where people actually live, and live well. Because of the casinos and the tourists, there is plenty of work and plenty to spend your money on - just make sure you remember to save enough to get some R&R when you've had enough!

## Some Las Vegas facts...

★ Vegas has got the most hotel rooms in the world.
★ About 4,000 people move to Vegas every month!
★ Over 100,000 couples get married in Vegas each year.
★ The Hoover Dam is 660 feet thick at the base, 1,244 feet across, 726 feet high, and wide enough for a two lane highway at the crest. It was built from steel, rock and more than seven million tons of concrete - enough to pave a two lane road from New York to San Francisco. Wow!

## Top things to do in Las Vegas

★ Stay cool in one of the billion dollar casinos on Las Vegas Boulevard (the Strip) but DON'T put your hard earned gap year money in the hands of fate!
★ Spend your day watching the no frill, walk-in weddings at the Cupid's wedding chapel - aren't the doves and roses tempting you just a bit?
★ Take in one of the endless neon, cheesy theme shows (and hopefully survive to tell the tale).
★ They say you don't have to be a trekkie to enjoy 'Star Trek: The Experience' but if the Starfleet Academy means anything to you, then this is particularly your thing.
★ Take a tour, with the other 3,000 people daily, to the BIG Hoover Dam. As one of the most popular day trip destinations in America, it's definitely worth seeing.
★ And if all that doesn't get you excited, how about a breath-taking helicopter ride over the Grand Canyon.

## Las Vegas Visitor Information Center

▤ 3150 Paradise Road
☎ 702 892 7575
⬠ www.lasvegas24hours.com

# las vegas

## Getting there

Las Vegas-McCarran International Airport is only five miles and 20 minutes away from Las Vegas and just $1.25 on the bus.

There's no railway station in Las Vegas but the Greyhound bus station is on 200 S Main Street.

## Getting around

The best way to see Las Vegas is by car. But there are also the buses - a one way ticket is $1.25.

## Accommodation

## Hostels

★ **Crest Budget Inn**, 207 N 6th Street - 702 384 1441 or 800 777 2566
★ **Glass Pool Inn**, 4611 Las Vegas Boulevard S - 702 738 6800 or 800 527 7118
★ **Las Vegas International Hostel**, 1208 Las Vegas Boulevard South - 702 385 9955, info@lasvegashostel.com, www.lasvegashostel.com
★ **Ogden House**, 651 E Ogden Avenue - 702 385 5200 or 800 634 6703
★ **USA Hostels** - Las Vegas, 1322 Fremont Street - 800 550 8958, lasvegas@usahostels.com, www.usahostels.com

## Camping

★ **American Campgrounds**, 3440 Las Vegas Boulevard - 702 643 1222
★ **Fam Camp**, 490 7 Fam Camp - 702 643 3060
★ **Las Vegas Int RV Resort**, 6900 E Russell Road - 702 433 1596
★ **Oasis Las Vegas RV Resort**, 2711 W Windmill Lane - 702 260 2020

## Work

Vegas means casinos, casinos mean tourists and tourists mean big business and big money. Vegas is a town built on service and with every casino, hotel, bar and restaurant desperate to outdo the other, they are always looking for extra hands to make the difference. Look smart, professional, customer-friendly and ready to attract a whole load of money for the people you want to work for, and you'll go a long way.

## Bar work

★ **Cafe Heidelberg German Deli**, 610 E Sahara Avenue - 702 731 5310

★ **Crown & Anchor Pub**, 1350 E Tropicana Avenue - 702 739 8676

★ **Fado Irish Pubs**, Green Valley Ranch, 2300 Paseo Verde Parkway, Henderson - 702 407 8691

★ **JC Wooloughan's Irish Pub**, 221 N Rampart Boulevard - 702 869 7777

★ **Mad Dogs & Englishmen Pub**, 515 Las Vegas Boulevard - 702 382 7301

★ **Schuler's Roadhouse**, 4755 Spring Mountain Road - 702 252 7427

★ **Sean Patrick's**, 8255 W Flamingo Road - 702 227 9793

## Casino work

★ **Bally's - Las Vegas**, 3645 Las Vegas Boulevard South - 702 967 4299

★ **Bellagio Employment Center** - 702 693 8222 or 702 693 8888

★ **Caesars Palace**, 3570 Las Vegas Boulevard South - 702 731 7110 or 800 634 6001

★ **Circus Circus Hotel**, 2880 Las Vegas Boulevard South - 702 734 0410

★ **Excalibur Hotel & Casino**, 3850 Las Vegas Boulevard South - 702 597 7100

★ **Golden Nugget Las Vegas Employment Center** - 702 386 8245 or 702 386 8181

★ **Luxor Las Vegas**, 3900 Las Vegas Boulevard South - 702 262 4732 or 800 777 2771

# las vegas

★ **MGM Mirage**, 3600 Las Vegas Boulevard South - 702 693 7111
★ **New York New York Hotel & Casino**, 3790 Las Vegas Boulevard South - 702 740 6969 or 800 693 6763
★ **Primm Valley Resorts** - 31900 South Las Vegas Boulevard, Primm - 702 679 5560 or 702 679 5627
★ **Sahara Hotel,** 2535 Las Vegas Boulevard South - 702 737 2111 or 888 737 2111
★ **Stardust Hotel & Casino**, 3000 Las Vegas Boulevard South - 702 732 6111 or 800 824 6033

## Office work

★ **A Bright Solution Employment Center**, 2860 East Flamingo Road - 702 646 8080
★ **Accountants Inc Temporary & Permanent Personnel Service**, 3770 Howard Hughes Parkway - 702 734 1110
★ **Add-A-Temp**, 3505 East Flamingo Road - 702 451 2331
★ **Adecco**, 1050 East Flamingo Road - 702 731 2267, info@adeccona.com, www.USAdecco.com
★ **Call Center Staffing Solutions**, 4220 South Maryland Parkway - 702 732 2484
★ **Eastridge Temps** - 702 732 8861
★ **Kelly Services**, 1160 North Town Center Drive - 702 255 4877
★ **Manpower**, 3068 East Sunset Road - 702 363 2626
★ **Remedy the Intelligent Temporary Service**, 3585 East Flamingo Road - 702 369 0292
★ **Snelling Personnel Services**, 1850 East Flamingo Road Site 105 - 702 731 9988, LasVegas@snelling.com
★ **Title Temps**, 2820 West Charleston Boulevard - 702 247 4455
★ **United Temps**, 900 Karen Avenue - 702 791 2629
★ **Universal Temps**, 2000 South Jones Boulevard - 702 364 0725

## Communications

### Internet cafés

★  **At Quick Page Café.com**, 3395 S Jones Boulevard - 702 365 8888

★  **Internet Café**, 3743 Las Vegas Boulevard - 702 736 4782

★  **Internet Café of Las Vegas**, 320 E Charleston Boulevard - 702 897 0142

### Library

★  **Las Vegas-Clark County Library**, 833 Las Vegas Boulevard - 702 734 7323

## Emergencies

**University Medical Center**

✉  1800 W Charleston Boulevard

☎  702 383 2000

**Desert Spring Hospital**

✉  2075 E Flaming Road

☎  702 733 8800

**Las Vegas Metro Police**

✉  400 Steward Avenue

☎  702 795 3111

**south west**

# phoenix

## Why Phoenix?

Phoenix is a city that seems to be constantly growing. More and more of the desert is being consumed by the city. It's hot and sunny all the year round and the city glistens with office blocks, shopping malls, new resorts and golf courses, all keeping the tourists pouring in. If you can stand the heat and the overwhelming modernity of the place, then Phoenix is an exciting, developing place to live and work in.

## Some Phoenix facts
★     The skies in Phoenix are clear 59% of the time!
★     Phoenix is the United States' sixth largest city with a population of nearly 1.3 million
★     Phoenix has an average annual rainfall of 7.66 inches, an average annual high temperature of 85 degrees and averages 300 sun-filled days per year.

## Top things to do in Phoenix
★     Get all touchy feely at the Arizona Science Center (600 E Washington Street) where you can explore 350 hands-on exhibits, a five story theatre and a planetarium.
★     Take a workshop in ethnobotany (and then tell us what it means!) at the Desert Botanical Gardens. They boast the world's largest collection of arid-land plants as well as having a stack of info on conservation, desert living, plants and people of the Sonoran Desert. Hot stuff!
★     Take a van or off-road tour to the edge of the Grand Canyon… and if you're looking for something a bit more extreme, sign up for a Grand Canyon raft trip. Aaaargh!
★     For a free day out, you can take a trip to the Hoo-hoogam Ki Museum on the Salt River Reservation. A fascinating insight into Pima and Maricopa culture and the history of the Salt River Indian Community. And authentic food too!
★     For some genuinely funny moments, we recommend a night at the Tempe Improv (930 East University Drive) - an improvisation comedy show with nationally known comedians.

**Greater Phoenix Convention & Tourism Bureau**
🖃     400 E Van Buren Street, Suite 600
☎     602 254 6500
⌂     www.visitphoenix.com

## Getting there

Sky Harbour International Airport is close to Phoenix. The Red Line and No 13 buses run frequently between the airport and city centre.

If you are arriving by train you need to get off at Maricopa station as Amtrak don't have a station there any more.

If you're coming by bus, the Greyhound bus station is south of downtown.

## Getting around

There are two bus companies that run Phoenix public transport - DASH and Valley Metro. Valley Metro has 12 local bus routes and DASH looks after the services for the downtown Phoenix. A one-way ticket on either is $1.25 and ten-ride ticket is only $12. If you are planning to stay longer in the desert city it's better to buy a monthly pass for $34.

## Accommodation

### Hostels

★    **Home Exchange**, 310 798 3864, www.homeexhange.com
★    **The Youth Hostel**, The Metcalf House, 1026 North 9th Street - 602 254 9803

### Camping

★    **North Phoenix Camping Ground**, 2550 N Louise Drive - 602 869 8189
★    **Pecan Grove Park**, 333 N 27 Avenue - 602 258 3153
★    **Pioneer Park**, 1946 W Morningside Drive - 602 262 4543

# phoenix

## Work

## Bar work

- ★ **Altos**, 5029 W 44th Street - 602 808 0890
- ★ **The American Lounge**, 1514 N 7th Avenue - 602 256 9705
- ★ **Amsterdam**, 718 N Central Avenue - 603 253 6122
- ★ **Baja Reds Cantina**, 5122 E McDowell Road - 602 286 9250
- ★ **Blue Ox**, 2401 N 32nd Street - 602 955 3249
- ★ **The Bunk House Saloon**, 4428 North 7th - 602 200 9154
- ★ **Charlie's**, 777 W Mariposa Street- 602 264 1065
- ★ **Downtown**, 702 N Central Avenue - 602 258 8343
- ★ **Finish Line**, 1724 W Bell Road - 602 863 2025
- ★ **Hard Rock Café**, 2621 E Camelback Road - 602 956 3669
- ★ **Harley's Club 155**, 155 West Camelback Road - 602 274 8505
- ★ **Hot Shots**, 2929 N 16th Street - 602 549 2929
- ★ **Jonny's MC's**, 138 West Camelback Road - 602 266 0875
- ★ **North Shore Beach Club**, 15626 N 32nd Street - 602 493 8622
- ★ **Office Lounge**, 3501 N 43rd Avenue - 602 269 4883
- ★ **Paradise Lounge**, 4541 E Cactus Lounge - 602 953 2993
- ★ **Pati's Pub**, 12820 N 19th Avenue - 602 943 7978
- ★ **Rada's Lounge**, 3632 W McDowell Road - 602 278 5843
- ★ **Rhythm Room**, 1019 E Indian School Road - 602 265 4842
- ★ **Rodeo Nights**, 4029 N 33rd Avenue - 602 279 2800
- ★ **Roscoe's on 7th**, 4531 N 7th Street - 602 285 0833

## Office work

- ★ **Blaine Personnel Service**, 1202 E Missouri Avenue - 602 222 9910
- ★ **Far Western Temp-Perm**, 8111 N 9 Avenue - 602 943 5026
- ★ **Instaff Personnel**, 3057 W Indian School Road - 602 265 5990
- ★ **Kelly Services**, 3034 N 3rd Street - 602 264 0717
- ★ **Sharp Staffing**, 2340 W Thomas Road - 602 252 3223

## Hotel work

- ★ **American Suites**, 10838 N 25th Avenue - 602 997 8800
- ★ **Arizona Biltmore Resort Hotel**, 24 Street E Missouri Avenue - 602 955 6600
- ★ **Downtown Holiday Inn Express**, 620 North Sixth Street - 602 452 2020
- ★ **Crown Plaza Downtown**, 100 North First Street - 602 333 000
- ★ **Crown Plaza North**, 2532 West Peoria Avenue - 603 943 2341
- ★ **Embassy Suites Hotel**, 1515 N 44th Street - 602244 8800
- ★ **Four Point Barceló Hotel**, 10220 N Metro Parkway - 602 331 9810
- ★ **Grand Bay Hotel and Resort**, 11811 N Tatum Boulevard - 602 953 6400
- ★ **Hilton Suites Phoenix Plaza**, 10 E Thomas Road - 602 222 111
- ★ **Holiday Inn Express Hotel and Suites**, 3401 E University Drive - 602 453 9900
- ★ **Hotel San Carlos**, 202 North Central Avenue - 602 253 4121
- ★ **Hyatt Hotels and Resorts**, 122 N 2nd Street - 602 252 1234
- ★ **Phoenix Marriott Airport**, 1101 North 44th Street - 602 273 7373
- ★ **Premier Inns**, 10402 Clack Canyon Freeway - 602 943 2371
- ★ **Royal Palmas Resort and Spa**, 5200 East Camelback Road - 602 840 3610
- ★ **Sheraton**, 5594 W Wild Horse Pass Boulevard - 602 225 0100
- ★ **Spring Hill Suites Phoenix Downtown**, 802 East Van Buren Street - 602 307 9929

## Language schools

- ★ **Berliz Language Center**, 3333 E Camelback Road Suite 160 - 602 468 9494

south west

## Communications

### Internet cafés
★     **Gypsy Java**, 3321 E Bell Road
★     **The@Café**, South East Corner of Alma Street
★     **Inn House Video & Cypercafé**, 126 A Coffee Pot Drive Sedona

### Libraries
★     **Acacia**, 750 E Townley Avenue - 602 262 4636
★     **Burton Park Central Library**, 1221 N Central Avenue - 602 2624636
★     **Century**, 1750 E Highland Avenue - 602 262 4636
★     **Desert Sage**, 7602 W Encanto Boulevard
★     **Juniper**, 1825 W Union Hills Drive

## Emergencies

**Phoenix Memorial Hospital**
▤     17201 S 7th Avenue
☎     602 258 5111

**Arizona State Hospital**
▤     2500 E Van Buren Street
☎     602 273 1115

**Police Headquarters**
▤     620 W Washington Street
☎     602 262 7626

Hard work and the pioneering spirit unite the people of these very different areas. From the industrial and musical powerhouse of 'Motown' Detroit to the harsh beauty of Denver and Colorado, the turbulent past and dynamic future of Chicago to the rich cultural heritage of St Louis, there's an incredible range of people and places to see. Whatever you're looking for in terms of work and travel experiences, it's hard to find an area as diverse.

image courtesy of Colorado Toursim Office

# chicago

## Why Chicago?

Chicago is another of the most instantly recognisable cities in the US. It is a city that has a powerful image, built on its colourful history of Prohibition-busting gangsters and jazz and blues musicians as well as its modern day reputation for innovation and commercial excellence. It's great to look at too, with some of the world's tallest skyscrapers - the Sears Towers and the John Hancock Center - as well as loads of fine old buildings. Chicago is the cultural capital of America's Midwest, home to a mind-boggling array of great bars, restaurants, live music, top shows, world class museums and art galleries.

## Some Chicago facts...
★ The city has 15 miles of beaches.
★ Chicago has got the world's largest public library.
★ It's also got the world's biggest biscuit factory!

## Top things to do in Chicago
★ Take in a game at McCormick Place, home of the Chicago Bears (football) and the Chicago Fire (soccer).
★ Every June is Pride Fest time - continuous entertainment, food and drink for festival-goers. There's one stage with dance music and one with top-name, local, regional and national musical headliners.
★ Not to be outdone, there's also the Weed Street Summerfest which focuses on the newest, brightest, most evolved nightclub entertainment in Chicago. Area nightclubs team up to put on this two day party of great music, food and beer. Definitely worth a look.
★ And not forgetting the African/Caribbean International Festival of Life every July including rhythm and blues, gospel, calypso and world beat. Can you manage it all?!
★ Get cultural in River North - they say it's the 'chic' district with art galleries that rank second only to Manhattan's Soho area. All very trendy!

## Chicago Convention & Tourism Bureau
☎ 877 244 2246
🕸 www.choosechicago.com

## Getting there

Chicago O'Hare International Airport is 18 miles from hectic Chicago. Transport to and from is efficient and fast with shuttle buses, taxis, trains and airport buses running between the airport and the city really regularly.

The Airport Express bus departs every 15 minutes. The first bus goes at 6.00am and the last one leaves the airport at 11.30pm. The fare is around $18.00. Though the train is cheaper, the blue line runs to city centre for just $1.25 and it takes 45 minutes.

Amtrak trains arrive at Union Station which is on Canal Street (between Adams Street and Jackson Boulevard). The Greyhound bus station is on the west side of the city - 630 Harrison Street.

## Getting around

Chicago Transit Authority (CTA) sorts out Chicago's public transport. The El is a comprehensive rail system that stretches around almost all of the city. One way on an El train costs $1.50 while a 30-day ticket is $75. Where the El trains don't go, the buses will.

## Accommodation

## Hostels

★ **Arlington International House**, 616 West Arlington Place - 773 929 5380
★ **Chicago International Hostel**, 6318 North Winthrop Avenue - 773 262 1011, chicagohostel@hotmail.com, www.chicagointernationalhostel.com
★ **Chicago Summer Hostel**, 731 S Plymouth Court - 312 327 5350
★ **Fat Johnnies Last Resort Home Hostel**, 2822 West 38th Place - 773 254 0836
★ **HI Chicago**, 24 East Congress Parkway - 312 360 0300

rockies plains & lakes

# chicago

## Work

Chicago has always been a city that knows how to make money - it's what made it the commercial powerhouse it is today. Companies are always on the lookout for workers with the right skills and it's worth putting yourself about a bit in your search for temporary work.

## Bar & restaurant work

★ **Abbey Pub & Restaurant**, 3420 West Grace Street - 773 478 4408
★ **Barleycorn John Memorial Pub**, 658 West Belden Avenue - 773 348 8899
★ **Cardozos Pub**, 170 West Washington Street - 312 236 1573
★ **Davenport's**, 1383 N Milwaukee - 773 278 1830
★ **FADO Irish Pub**, 100 West Grand Avenue - 312 836 0066
★ **Irish Abbey Pub**, Grace And Elston - 773 478 4408
★ **The Irish Oak**, 3511 N Clark Street - 773 935 6669
★ **Millers Pub & Restaurant**, 134 South Wabash Avenue - 312 263 4988
★ **The Phillip Kling Brewing Company**, 5640 North Kenmore Avenue - 773 561 1888
★ **Timothy O'Toole's Pub**, 622 North Fairbanks Court - 312 642 5282

## Hotel work

- ★ **Drake Hotel**, 140 East Walton Street - 312 787 2200
- ★ **Fairmont Hotel**, 200 N Columbus Drive - 312 565 8000
- ★ **Four Seasons Hotel Chicago**, 120 East Delaware Place at 900 N Michigan Avenue - 312 280 8800
- ★ **Hotel Inter Continental**, 505 N Michigan Avenue - 312 944 4100
- ★ **Hyatt On Printers Row**, 500 South Dearborn Street - 312 986 1234
- ★ **Omni Ambassador East**, 1301 North State Parkway - 312 787 7200
- ★ **Palmer House Hilton**, 17 East Monroe Street - 312 726 7500
- ★ **Radisson Hotel & Suites Chicago Downtown**, 160 East Huron Street - 312 787 2900
- ★ **Raphael Hotel**, 201 East Delaware Place - 312 943 5000
- ★ **Regal Knickerbocker Hotel**, 163 East Walton Street - 312 751 8100
- ★ **Renaissance Chicago Hotel**, 1 West Wacker Drive - 312 372 7200
- ★ **Ritz Carlton Hotel Chicago**, 160 E Pearson Street - 312 266 1000
- ★ **Sheraton Chicago Hotel & Towers**, 301 East North Water Street - 312 464 1000
- ★ **Silversmith**, 10 South Wabash Avenue - 312 372 7696
- ★ **Swissotel Chicago**, 323 E Wacker Drive - 312 565 0565
- ★ **Talbott Hotel**, 20 East Delaware Place - 312 944 4970
- ★ **The Tremont Hotel**, 100 E Chestnut Street - 312 751 1900
- ★ **Westin Chicago River North**, 320 N Dearborn Avenue - 312 744 1900
- ★ **Wyndham Chicago**, 633 N Saint Clair Street - 312 573 0300

**rockies plains & lakes**

# chicago

## Office work

- ★ **Adecco Employment Services**, 123 West Madison Street - 312 782 1014, info@adeccona.com, www.USAdecco.com
- ★ **Bevelle Temporary** - 312 807 3850
- ★ **Climatemp**, 1427 East 60th Street - 773 955 8047
- ★ **Express Personnel Services**, 5526 North Milwaukee Avenue - 773 725 0100
- ★ **First Temporary Services**, 28 East Jackson Boulevard - 312 939 7112
- ★ **Loftus & Omeara Temporary Service**, 166 East Superior Street - 312 944 2102
- ★ **Manpower**, 8745 West Higgins Road - 773 693 2291
- ★ **Midwest Temps**, 2546 West North Avenue - 773 252 7777
- ★ **New OFC Temps**, 1 East Wacker Drive - 312 923 0054
- ★ **Officeteam**, 205 North Michigan Avenue - 847 885 6228
- ★ **PC Temps**, 230 North Michigan Avenue - 312 855 9511
- ★ **Protemp Temporaries**, 230 East Ohio Street - 312 751 0444
- ★ **Randstad**, 212 E Ohio Street - 312 266 1432
- ★ **Right Temporaries**, 3960 West 95th Street - 708 636 6800
- ★ **Selectemps**, 2971 South Archer Avenue - 773 890 1868
- ★ **Temporary Professionals** - 773 622 1202
- ★ **Temps Unlimited**, 70 East Lake Street - 312 263 0491
- ★ **United Temps**, 2500 South Drake Avenue - 773 521 7005
- ★ **Webster Temporary Service**, 108 West Hubbard Street - 312 329 9605
- ★ **WW Temps**, 2457 North Milwaukee Avenue - 773 394 9912

## Language school work

- ★ **American English Academy**, 180 N Michigan Avenue - 312 853 0434
- ★ **American Top English**, 1735 N Ashland Avenue - 773 489 3202
- ★ **Berlitz Language Center**, 2 N La Salle Street - 312 782 6820
- ★ **English Language Education**, 310 S Michigan Avenue - 312 986 9798
- ★ **Turner Drew Language Academy**, 9300 S Princeton Avenue - 773 535 5720

## Communications

### Internet cafés

★    **American Internet Café**, 2457 W Peterson Avenue -
773 728 4940

★    **Cybernet Café**, 4740 N Cumberland Avenue - 773 625 6710

★    **Future World**, 1744 E 55th Street - 773 256 1570

★    **Global Internet Café**, 4467 W Lawrence Avenue -
773 7777 5557

★    **Internet Café of Chicago**, 5809 N Lincoln Avenue -
773 784 7744

★    **Off The Wall Wireless Café**, 1904 W North Avenue -
312 702 0000

## Emergencies

**British Consulate-General**
✉    13th Floor, The Wrigley Building, 400 N Michigan Avenue
☎    312 970 3800

**University of Chicago Hospital**
✉    5841 S Maryland Avenue
☎    773 02 1000

**Mercy Hospital**
✉    2525 S Michigan Avenue
☎    312 567 2600

**Chicago Police Department**
✉    5151 N Milwaukee Avenue
☎    773 742 4480

**rockies plains & lakes**

# denver

## Why Denver?

Denver is one of the most spectacular cities in the US, set in the foothills of the Rockies. The city has skyscrapers and Victorian buildings, beautiful parks and loads of places to shop. Denver is a fresh, healthy and thriving city with great weather and plenty of opportunities to get involved in all kinds of outdoor activities. Colorado is one of the most beautiful states in the US with two national parks and around 30 state parks - a lot are within easy reach of Denver itself.

## Some Denver facts...
★     The cheeseburger was invented in Denver.
★     The city has a population of over half a million.
★     Denver has got more urban parks than any other American city.
★     Denver started as a gold mining camp in 1859.
★     Denver brews more beer than any other city in the nation!
★     The city has the largest city park system in the nation, with 205 parks inside city limits and 20,000 acres in the mountains

## Top things to do in Denver...
(Not to be confused with 'things to do in when Denver when you're dead'!)
★     Take in the view from Colorado's State Capitol Rotunda. And if you stand on the 15th step on the west side of the State Capitol Building you'll be exactly one mile high - not a lot of people know that!
★     Tour the Coors brewery for free! (but don't forget that this is the US - you will have to be over 21 to do it)
★     Go for a hike in the Rocky Mountain National Park - with over 355 miles of trails to choose from, you'll hopefully find the right one for your stamina. And if you're really serious about it, you can hike and camp to your heart's content.
★     Take in a performance at the Denver Center for the Performing Arts. Or just wander round the historic buildings, art deco designs and 80-foot clear glass arch in awe. And if that's not enough, get this - it covers four city blocks of downtown.

## Denver Metro Convention & Visitors Bureau
▭     1555 California, Suite 300
☎     800 233 6837
⬟     www.denver.org

## Getting there

Denver International Airport is 23 miles away from the city centre. British Airways, Air Canada and United Airlines fly there frequently.

You can get a shuttle bus from right outside the baggage claim area to get into the city. They run from the first morning flight until the last one in the evening.

The Amtrak train arrives at the beautiful Old Union Station at 1701 Wynkoop Street. The Greyhound bus station is close by at 1055 19th Street.

## Getting around

The RTD light rail runs from suburban Denver to the city centre. If you can't get where you want to on the light rail you can hop on to an RTD bus. A one-way ticket with any RTD services is $1.55 and a ten-ride ticket is $9.25. You can buy tickets from local Safeway and King Soopers stores, RTD transit stations and ticket vending machines.

## Accommodation

## Hostels

★ **Denver International Hostel**, 630 E 16 Avenue - 303 832 9996
★ **Hostel of the Rocky Mountains**, 1530 Downing - 303 861 7777
★ **Melbourne International Youth Hostel**, 607 22 Denver - 303 292 6386

## Camping

★ **Arche's Poudre River Resort**, 33021 Poudre Canyon - 888 822 0588
★ **Chief Hosa**, 27661 Genesee Drive, Golden - 303 380 4672, www.chiefhosa.com
★ **Denver East/Strasburg KOA**, PO Box 597, Strasburg - 303 622 9274

rockies plains & lakes

# denver

## Work

The Mile High City has more than enough cool shops, restaurants and funky nightlife to not only keep you entertained but also to help pay your rent as well. Check out our list below and ask around to see if they've got any jobs going. Try and get in touch with them in advance of your arrival in Denver - it makes you look efficient and it will ease your worries too!

## Bar work

★ **Arabian Bar**, 3360 Navajo - 303 480 9435
★ **Blue 67**, 1475 Lawrence Street - 303 260 7505
★ **Campus Lounge**, 701 S University Boulevard - 303 722 9696
★ **Citrus**, 1701 Wynkood - 303 573 1121
★ **City Limits**, 7950 E Mississippi Avenue - 303 368 4959
★ **Fado's Irish Bar**, 1735 19th Street - 303 297 0066
★ **Falling Rock Tap House**, 1919 Blake Street - 303 293 8447
★ **Funky Buddha**, 776 Lincoln Street - 303 832 5075
★ **Giggling Grizzly**, 1320 20th Street - 303 297 8300
★ **The Hornet**, 76 Broadway - 303 777 4528
★ **My Brother's Bar**, 2376 15th Street - 303 455 9991
★ **Nallen's Irish Bar**, 1429 Market Street - 303 572 0667
★ **Pint's Pub**, 221 W 13th Avenue - 303 534 7543
★ **Red Room**, 320 E Colfax Avenue - 303 830 7050
★ **Seven South**, 7 South Broadway - 303 744 0513
★ **Skylark Lounge**, 58 Broadway - 303 722 7844
★ **Street of London Pub**, 1502 E Colfax Avenue - 303 861 9103
★ **William's Tavern**, 421 E 17th Avenue - 303 861 9813

## Hotel work

* **Continental Hotel**, 2601 Zuni - 303 433 6677
* **Courtyard by Marriott**, 7415 E 41 Avenue - 303 333 3303
* **Denver Marriott City Central**, 1710 California Street - 888 441 1294
* **Doubletree Hotel**, 3203 Quebec Street - 303 321 3333
* **Embassy Suites Hotel**, 7525 E Hampden Avenue - 303 696 6644
* **Executive Tower Inn**, 1405 Curtis Street - 303 571 0300
* **Four Points by Sheraton**, 1475 S Colorado Boulevard - 303 757 8797
* **Hawthorne Suites Hotel**, 500 1 S Ulster - 303 804 9900
* **Omni Interlocken Resort**, 500 Interlocken Boulevard- 303 438 6600
* **Ramada Inn North**, 1150 E Colfax Avenue - 303 831 7700
* **Renaissance Denver Hotel**, 3801 Quebec - 303 399 7500

## Office work

* **Denver Works**, 2828 N Speer Boulevard Suite 103 - 303 433 0300
* **Kelly Services**, 1625 Broadway - 303 623 6262
* **Link Staffing**, 565 E 70th Avenue Suite 1W - 303 286 8886
* **Manpower**, 1777 S Harrison - 303 758 2700
* **Office Alternatives**, 1600 Broadway - 303 861 1920
* **Office Team**, 1225 Seventeenth Street - 303 296 4900
* **Staff Works**, 5353 W Dartmouth Avenue - 303 756 4440
* **Tandem Staffing**, 66 Kalamath Street - 303 534 1316
* **Temporary Market**,. 600 17th Street - 303 295 2502
* **Today's Office Staffing** - 303 830 0022
* **Total Temporise**, 224 W 6 Avenue - 303 629 5433

rockies plains & lakes

## Language school work

★ **Berlitz Language Center**, 55 Madison Street - 303 399 8686,
www.berlitz.com

★ **Bridge International School**, 915 South Colorado Boulevard -
303 777 7783, www.ies-ed.com

★ **Colorado School of English**, 331 14th Street - 720 932 8900,
www.englishamerica.com

★ **ELS Language Center**, 333 Regis Boulevard - 303 480 1565,
www.els.com

★ **Expanded Learning**, 1571 Race Street - 303 333 3445,
www.expanded-learning.com

## Communications

## Internet cafés

★ **Café Netherworld**, 1278 Pennsylvania Street - 303 861 8638,
www.networld.com

★ **www.CowboyBar**, 1201 South Parker Road, Suite 104 -
303 368 4201, www.cowboybar.com

## Library

★ **Denver Public Library,** 10 W Fourteenth Avenue -
303 640 6200, www.denver.li.co.us

## Emergencies

**British Consulate**
✉ 1675 Broadway World Trade Centre, Suite 1030
☎ 303 592 5200

**University of Colorado Hospital**
✉ 4200 E 9th Avenue
☎ 303 327 0000

**Denver Police Department**
✉ 1331 Cherokee Street
☎ 720 913 6317
🕸 www.denvergov.org

## Why St Louis?

St Louis' great Gateway Arch reflects the city's history as an entrance to the new West. St Louis has had its boom times and its bad times, but it is a city with a rich heritage of pioneers - in industry and in music. St Louis has very culturally diverse neighbourhoods, allowing you to sample a great range of different foods and music. The city also has a thriving business community, giving you plenty of scope for finding work or work experience - it's a city with a proud and unique atmosphere of its own.

## Some St Louis facts...

★ The people of St Louis consume more barbecue sauce per head than anywhere else in the US.
★ St Louis was the place where 7-Up was invented.
★ Chuck Berry, Tina Turner, Miles Davis and peanut butter all came from St Louis!

## Top things to do in St Louis...

★ Look up in awe at the nation's tallest monument. The Gateway Arch is a mere 630ft towering over St Louis.
★ Do the grave tour - Bellefontaine Cemetery is home to William Clark, Thomas Hart Benton, James Eads, Adolphus Busch, Sara Teasdale. And Tennessee Williams, General William Tecumseh Sherman and Dred Scott can all be found at Calvary Cemetery.
★ Think of St Louis and think of Scott Joplin, the 'King of Ragtime'. You can visit Scott Joplin House where ragtime classics were composed and also find out all you need to know about Joplin's life and work.
★ Or you can wander for ever around Forest Park - it's the country's largest urban park.

**St Louis Convention & Visitors Commission**

✉ One Metropolitan Square, Suite 1100
☎ 800 325 7962
⌂ www.explorestlouis.com

rockies plains & lakes

# st louis

## Getting there

St Louis has a busy international airport with frequent flights from Canadian Air and Continental among others. The best way to get to the city centre is to jump onto a MetroLink train. A one way ticket costs $3.00 and the journey to the city centre takes around 25 minutes.

Arriving by train can be a breathtaking experience. St Louis' Old Union Station has been said to be the largest, most beautiful station in the US. The Union Station is downtown with the Greyhound bus station close by on 1450 N 13th Street.

## Getting around

The best way to get around in St Louis is to buy a MetroLink one day pass for $4. But if you don't want to get in stuck in downtown traffic, hire a bike. It's one of the most bike-friendly cities in America. And if you get tired of cycling, you can always take your bike on MetroLink buses for free.

## Accommodation

## Hostels

★ **Gateway Council of Hostelling**, 7187 Manchester Road - 314 644 4660

## Camping

★ **Cahokia RV Parque**, 4060 Mississippi Avenue - 681 332 7700
★ **Casino Queen RV Park**, 200 S Front Street - 800 747 0777
★ **Koa Granite City Camping**, 3157 W Chain of Rocks Road - 618 931 5160
★ **Pin Oak Creek RV Park**, 1302 Highway, Villa Ridge - 636 451 5656
★ **St Louis RV Park**, 900 N Jefferson Downtown - 314 241 3330
★ **Sundermeier RV Park**, 111 Transit Street St Charles - 636 940 0111
★ **Yogi Bear's Jellystone Resort at Six Flags**, 5300 Fox Creek Road - 636 938 5925

## Work

Live music and entertainment is a big thing in St Louis so here are some good places to start if you're looking for work in the clubs and bars. You might even get to meet Chuck Berry.

## Bar work

★ **Black Thorn Pub**, 3735 Wyoming Street - 314 776 0534
★ **Blue Moon Pub**, 2234 First Capitol Drive - 314 940 1819
★ **Bridgeton Pub**, 12207 Natural Bridge Road - 314 209 0470
★ **Eagle's Nest Pub**, 83 Charleston Square - 636 447 9895
★ **Elsher's**, 716 N. 1st Street - 314 421 0141
★ **Ferguson's Pub**, 2725 Mount Pleasant Street - 314 351 1466
★ **Grey Fox Pub**, 3503 S Spring Avenue - 314 742 2150
★ **Greyhan's Irish Pub**, 6413 W Main Street - 618 394 1300
★ **Growler's Pub**, 763 Old Rallas Road - 314 432 3110
★ **Hard Rock Café**, St Louis Union Station - 314 612 7625
★ **John D McGurks**, 1200 Russela Road - 314 776 8305
★ **Llywelyn's Pub**, 4747 McPherson Avenue - 314 361 3003
★ **Little Corner Pub**, 830 Brown Street - 618 465 1948
★ **Liquid**, 326 S. 21st Street - 314 241 6200
★ **Living Room**, 1014 Lolu Street - 314 588 9000
★ **Maggie's O'Brien's**, 2000 Market Street - 314 421 1388
★ **Mike & Min's**, 925 Geyer Avenue - 314 421 1655
★ **Off Broadway**, 3511 Lemp Avenue - 314 773 3363
★ **Planet Hollywood**, 800 North 3rd Street - 314 588 1717
★ **Soul Art Ale House**, 1732 S. Ninth Street - 314 436 7849
★ **Venice Café**, 1901 Pestalozzi Street - 314 772 5994
★ **Wild Country**, 17 Gateway, Collinsville - 618 346 6775

**rockies plains & lakes**

## Hotel work

* ★ **Baymont Inn & Suites West Port**, 12330 Dorsett Road - 314 878 1212
* ★ **Best Western, Western Park Hotel**, 2434 Old Dorsett Road - 314 291 8700
* ★ **Chase Park Plaza**, 232 N Kingshighway Boulevard - 314 633 3000
* ★ **Comfort Inn West Port**, 12031 Lackland Road - 314 878 1400
* ★ **Crown Hotel at the Casino Queen**, 200 S Front Street - 618 874 5000
* ★ **Drury Plaza**, 2 S 4th Street - 314 231 3003
* ★ **First Wester Inn**, 1951 Collinsville Road - 618 482 3088
* ★ **Holiday Inn, Hotel Forest Park**, 5915 Wilson Avenue - 314 645 0700
* ★ **La Quinta Inn Suites**, 11805 Lackland Road - 314 991 3262
* ★ **The Mayfair**, 806 St Charles Street - 972 915 7070
* ★ **Millennium Hotel**, 200 South Fourth Street - 314 241 9500
* ★ **Omni Majestic Hotel**, 1091 Pine Street - 314 436 2355
* ★ **Radisson Hotel & Suites**, 200 North Fourth Street - 314 621 8200
* ★ **Radisson Hotel Clayton**, 7750 Carondelet Avenue - 314 726 5400
* ★ **Ramada Inn**, 333 Washington Avenue - 314 621 7900
* ★ **Renaissance Grand Hotel**, 800 Washington Avenue - 314 621 19600
* ★ **Ritz-Carlton St Louis**, 100 Carondelet Plaza Street - 314 727 0099
* ★ **Sheraton Clayton Plaza Hotel**, 7730 Bonhomme Avenue - 314 863 0400
* ★ **Sheraton Four Points**, 310 South Fourth Street - 314 516 9300
* ★ **Sheraton St Louis**, City Central Hotel & Suites, 400 South 14th Street - 314 231 5007
* ★ **Wyndham Garden Hotel**, 1970 Graig Road - 314 205 8000

## Office work

★ **Accountemps**, 1 Metropolitan Square - 314 621 8888
★ **Express Personnel Service**, 1015 Locust Street -
314 621 8000
★ **Kelly Services**, 1 Metropolitan Square - 314 421 4111
★ **Manpower**, 200 N Broadway - 314 241 0700
★ **Millennium Staffing**, 515 N 6th Street - 314 621 7744
★ **Officeteam**, 1 Metropolitan Square - 314 621 8888
★ **Office Work Unlimited**, 9700 Mackenzie Road - 314 544 6867
★ **Sonderman Staffing Resources**, PO Box 31584 -
314 306 6527
★ **Spherion Office Professionals**, 12647 Olive Boulevard -
314 514 0202
★ **Today's Office Staffing**, 10 S Broadway - 314 241 3022

## Language school work

★ **Alliance Francaise School**, 8505 Delmar Boulevard -
314 432 0734
★ **Berlitz Language Centers**, 200 South Hanley Road -
314 721 1070
★ **East-West Language Service**, 606 North - 314 863 0255

rockies plains & lakes

# st louis

## Communications

## Internet café

★      **The Grind**, 56 Maryland Plaza - www.icon-stl.net

## Libraries

★      **Brenwood Public Library**, 2348 South Brentwood Boulevard - 314 962 4800
★      **Kirkwood Public Library**, 140 E Jefferson - 314 821 5770
★      **Maplewood Public Library**, 7601 Manchester Avenue - 314 781 2174
★      **Rock Hill Public Library**, 9620 Manchester Road - 314 962 4723
★      **St Louis Public Library**, 1301 Olive Street - 314 241 2288
★      **University Public Library**, 6701 Delmar Boulevard - 314 727 3150
★      **Valley Park Community Library**, 320 Benton Street - 636 225 5608

## Emergencies

**Barnes-Jewish Hospital**
🖃      216 S Kingshipway Boulevard
☎      314 454 7900

**St Louis Sheriff's Office**
🖃      10N Tucker Boulevard
☎      314 622 4766

Aloha! We've given Hawaii its very own section, because it's really very special. It's an idyllic place to live and work with perfect white beaches, tropical sun and the friendliest people you're ever likely to meet. There's work available, not just in Honolulu but also on farms on many of the islands. Organisations such as Alliances Abroad will place you on a farm in Hawaii, and give you all the support you need.

**Some Hawaii facts...**
* There are eight main islands - the biggest is called (creatively) the Big Island of Hawaii!
* The Hawaiian alphabet is quite straightforward - there's only 12 letters.
* 'Aloha' has many meanings and uses and has no real equivalent in English - it's kind of a combination of 'hello', goodbye', and 'I love you'.
* The islands are an incredible display of natural diversity - 21 of the world's 22 climactic zones are represented.

image courtesy of Hawaii Visitors & Convention Bureau

# honolulu

## Why Honolulu?

You shouldn't go to Honolulu looking for the essential authentic Hawaiian experience, but the islands' only major city is certainly a great place to live and work. The tourist beaches of Waikiki are just down the road and there are plenty of opportunities for temporary work in the resorts and in the city. It's a striking city to look at, with a stunning backdrop of extinct volcanoes towering over the skyscrapers, and the waterfront rimmed with beaches and crystal clear waters.

## Top things to do in Honolulu...

★   Worship Pele (not the Brazillian footballer but the Hawaiian fire goddess) at the Hawaii Volcanoes National Park, home to some of the world's most active volcanoes.

★   Explore the distinctive lifestyles of Tonga, Hawaii, Samoa, Fiji, Tahiti, Marquesas and New Zealand at the Polynesian Cultural Center. 27 million visitors to date must mean there's something there that's worth a peek...

★   Visit Pearl Harbor. Some of the site of the dawn attack on Pearl Harbor is now a National Memorial Park. If you're up for it, you can take in the USS Arizona Memorial, the USS Bowfin and the recently refurbished USS Missouri on the same day.

★   Nibble away on some 'pho' (a popular Vietnamese noodle dish) and a can of cold soy milk in downtown Honolulu while watching the old men playing Chinese chess or cards along the River Street Canal.

### Hawaii Visitors Bureau

🖃   Hibiscus Court, 4th Floor, Royal Hawaiian Shopping Center, Waikiki

☎   808 924 0266

## Getting there

Honolulu International Airport is one of the busiest hubs in the Pacific with the majority of trans-Pacific flights stopping off here. The airport also has several flights an hour to each of the major islands.

The extensive local bus service is called TheBus. Routes 19 and 20 run between the airport and Waikiki via downtown Honolulu. You need to bear in mind that it can sometimes be a bit tricky taking luggage on TheBus - peak times are the worst. So if you do have a lot of bags, you can try taking one of the more expensive shuttle buses. And there are also free shuttle buses run by some of the backpacker hostels that have beds to fill.

## Getting around

TheBus has around 80 routes covering the major urban areas of Pearl Harbor, Honolulu and Waikiki and much of the rest of the island. You may need to transfer in downtown Honolulu or the Ala Moana shopping mall but it's still a great service. A ticket on TheBus is $1 and you just ask the driver for a free transfer if you change! A four-day pass is a bargain $10.

image copyright: Hawaii Visitors & Convention Bureau

## Accommodation

### Hostels

★ **Banana Bungalow Waikiki Beach**, 2463 Kuhio Avenue - 808 924 5074

★ **Fernhurst YWCA**, 1040 Richards Street - 808 941 2231

★ **HI-Honolulu International Hostel**, 2323A Seaview Avenue - 808 946 0591

★ **HI-Waikiki**, 2417 Prince Edward Street - 808 926 8313

★ **Polynesian Hostel Beach Club**, 2584 Lemon Road - 808 922 1340, polynesian@hostelhawaii.com, www.hawaiihostels.com

★ **Waikiki Beachside Hostel**, 2556 Lemon Road, Suite B101 - 808 923 9566

### Camping

★ **Kwilts N KOA**, 1126 12th Aveste 101 - 808 735 2300, kwiltsnkoa@hawaii.rr.com

## Work

Life is pretty relaxed in Hawaii but the time is still going to come when you're going to have to find some work. Honolulu has plenty of opportunities for office work and the island's tourist resorts are always on the look out for people prepared to do a bit of temporary work. Waikiki Beach is a stone's throw from the centre of Honolulu, but if you look further afield there is work available in the more rural areas, from catering for tourists to working on farms.

## Bar work

★ **All Star Hawaii**, 2080 Kalakaua Avenue - 808 955 8326
★ **Angles Bar & Grill**, 2256 Kuhio Avenue - 808 922 3536
★ **Bedroq Bar & Grill**, 2535 Coyne Street - 808 942 8856
★ **Cafe Anasia, 2227 South Beretania Street** - 808 951 9295
★ **Cheerleaders Sports Bar & Grill**, Moanalua Shopping Center - 808 422 2242
★ **Da DAWG House**, 2330 Kalakaua Avenue - 808 924 3294
★ **Fort Street Bar & Grill**, 745 Fort Street Mall - 808 523 1500
★ **Laimu Grill & Bar**, 1020 Keeaumoku Street - 808 596 8001
★ **Murphy's Bar & Grill**, 2 Merchant Street - 808 531 0422
★ **Pipeline Cafe & Sports Bar**, 805 Pohukaina Street - 808 589 1999
★ **Shack Mililani**, 95-221 Kipapa Drive - 808 627 1561
★ **Sunset Grill**, 500 Ala Moana Boulevard Suite 1-A - 808 521 4409
★ **TJ's Sports Bar & Grill**, 600 Kapiolani Boulevard - 808 545 1114

## Farm work

★ **Del Monte Fresh Produce Hawaii**, PO Box 200, Kunia - 808 621 1320
★ **Gay & Robinson**, PO Box 156, Kaumakani - 808 335 3133
★ **Haleakala Ranch**, 529 Kealaloa Avenue, Makawao - 808 572 1800
★ **Maui Land & Pineapple Co**, PO Box 187, Kahului - 808 877 3351
★ **Parker Ranch**, 67-1435 Mamalahoa Highway, Kamuela - 808 885 7311

hawaii

# honolulu

## Hotel work

★ **Hilton Hawaiian Village Beach Resort & Spa**, 2005 Kalia Road - 808 949 4321

★ **Hyatt Regency Waikiki Resort & Spa**, 2424 Kalakaua Avenue - 808 923 1234

★ **Radisson Waikiki Prince Kuhio**, 2500 Kuhio Avenue - 808 922 0811

★ **Ramada Vacation Suites at Honolulu**, 431 Nohonani Street - 808 923 7336

★ **Royal Hawaiian Hotel**, 2259 Kalakaua Avenue - 808 931 8294

★ **Sheraton Moana Surfrider**, 2365 Kalakaua Avenue - 808 922 3111

★ **Sheraton Princess Kaiulani Hotel**, 120 Kaiulani Avenue - 808 922 5811

★ **Waikiki Beach Marriott Resort**, 2552 Kalakaua Avenue - 808 922 6611

## Office work

★ **Adecco**, 1001 Bishop Street - 808 486 9696
★ **Bluestar**, 801 Alakea Street - 808 526 1768
★ **Manpower**, 737 Bishop Street - 808 524 3630
★ **Norrell Temporary Services**, 201 Merchant - 808 531 9700
★ **Spherion**, 1440 Kapiolani Boulevard - 808 942 2333
★ **Temporary Help Services**, 1406 Colburn Street - 808 832 0050

## Language school work

★ **Institute of Intensive English**, 2255 Kuhio Avenue - 808 924 2117

★ **Nacos International Inc**, 765 Amana Stste 507 - 808 946 0579

★ **Pacific International Language School**, 1451 South King Stste 301A - 808 946 8485

## Communications

### Internet cafés

★  **Coco's Internet Café**, 2310 Kuhio Avenue #19 -
808 922 8500, www.coconetcafe.com

★  **Coffee Cove Online**, Puck's Alley, 2600 South King Street -
www.coffeecove.com

★  **Coffee Haven**, Kilohana Square, 1026 Kapahulu Avenue -
808 732 2090, www.coffee-haven.com

★  **Fishbowl Internet Café**, 2463 Kuhio Avenue - 808 922 7562,
www.fishbowlinternet.com

### Library

★  **Hawaii State Library**, 478 South King Street - 808 586 3500

## Emergencies

**Queen's Medical Center**

🖃  1301 Punchbowl Street

☎  808 538 9011

**Hawaii Poison Center**

☎  808 941 4411

**Honolulu Police Department**

🖃  801 South Beretania Street

🖱  hpd@honolulupd.org

🕸  www.honolulupd.org

hawaii

# web directory

## Accommodation
www.hostelworld.com
www.bookhostels.com
www.camping.about.com
www.hiayh.org
www.hostelhandbook.com
www.vipbackpackers.com
www.yha.org.uk

## Airlines
www.aa.com
www.airfrance.com
www.americawest.com
www.ba.com
www.cathaypacific.com
www.delta.com
www.flybmi.com
www.klm.com
www.nwa.com
www.qantas.com.au
www.southwest.com
www.ual.com
www.usairways.com
www.worldair.com

## Austin
www.austinchronicle.com
www.austinlinks.com
www.austinwebpage.com
www.ci.austin.tx.us
www.boulevards.com/austin
www.experienceaustin.com

## Backpacker guides
www.bootsnall.com
www.crazydogtravel.com
www.freetravelguides.com
www.gapwork.com
www.lonelyplanet.com
http://travel.roughguides.com/default.html

## Banks
www.bankofamerica.com
www.bankone.com
www.chase.com
www.citibank.com
www.usbank.com

## Boston
www.boston.com
www.boston-massachusetts.com
www.boston-online.com
www.bostonusa.com
www.digitalcity.com/boston
www.hostelboston.com
www.mfa.org/home.htm
www.visitboston.org

## Bus travel
www.adventurebus.com
www.ameribus.com
www.greentortoise.com
www.greyhound.com
www.theant.com
www.travelpackusa.com

## Camping
www.campnetamerica.com
www.campusa.com
www.freecampgrounds.com
www.gocampingamerica.com
www.koakampgrounds.com
www.reserveusa.com
www.rvpark.com
www.trailerlife.com

## Car hire
www.alamo.com
www.avis.com
www.dollar.com
www.hertz.com
www.thrifty.com

## Chicago
www.chicago.il.org
www.ci.chi.il.us/Tourism
http://egov.cityofchicago.org/city/webportal/home.do
www.mcachicago.org
metromix.chicagotribune.com

# web directory

www.newcitychicago.com/chicago/index.html
www.theskydeck.com

## Communications
www.attwireless.com
www.cheapest-phone-calls.com
www.cingular.com
www.superpages.com
www.yellowbook.com

## Currency
www.oanda.com

## Denver
www.artstozoo.org
www.buzz-denver.com
www.denver.org
www.denver.com
www.denvergov.org
www.denverpost.com
http://dodenver.com
www.milehighcity.com

## Disabled travellers
www.access-able.com

## Driving
www.autodriveaway.com
www.drivingabroad.co.uk
www.linkinone.com/rent-car-USA.html
www.movecars.com
www.roadsideamerica.com
www.usembassy.org.uk/cons_web/visa/us/drive.htm

## Employment
www.aboutjobs.com
www.adecco.com
www.adventurejobs.co.uk
www.aplus-summerjobs.com
www.bestjobsus.com
www.coolworks.com
www.freeradicals.co.uk

www.internjobs.com
www.jobbankusa.com
www.jobjester.com
www.jobsearch.about.com
www.monster.com
www.net-temps.com
www.petersons.com
www.resortjobs.com
www.summerjobs.com
www.teacherjobs.com
www.us.manpower.com

## Flight agents
www.cheapflights.co.uk
www.ebookers.com
www.expedia.co.uk
www.flights4less.co.uk
www.flightmapping.com
www.uk-flights-directory.co.uk

## Health
www.boots.co.uk
www.fco.gov.uk
www.masta.org

## Gay & lesbian
www.gayamerica.com
www.gayscape.com
www.gayellowpages.com
www.queery.com

## Honolulu
www.co.honolulu.hi.us
www.hawaii.com
www.honolulu-festival.com
www.honoluluweekly.com
www.honolulu.worldweb.com
www.honoluluzoo.org
www.visit-oahu.com

## Insurance
www.navigatortravel.co.uk

# web directory

## Internet cafés
www.cybercaptive.com
www.cyberiacafe.net/cyberia/guide
/ccafe.htm
www.netcafeguide.com/USA.htm

## Las Vegas
www.goingtovegas.com
www.lasvegas.com
www.lasvegascitylife.com
www.lasvegasweekly.com
www.lvol.com
www.nv-lasvegas.com

## Los Angeles
www.kasbah.com/guides/los_
angeles_editorial.htm
www.lacvb.com
www.lasightseeingcruises.com/
topics/sightseeing-tours
www.latourist.com
www.losangeles.com
www.pubclub.com/losangeles/
preparty.htm
www.seeing-stars.com

## Maps
www.city.net/regions/usa/maps
www.mapblast.com
www.mapquest.com
www.maptown.com
www.mapsworldwide.com
www.omnimap.com
www.pathfinder.com

## Miami
www.boulevards.com/miami
www.ci.miami.fl.us
www.gmcvb.com/Index.asp
http://miami.nightguide.com
www.miamivr.com/Events.htm
www.visitmiamibeach.us/
mrmiamibeach/home.jsp

## New Orleans
www.experienceneworleans.com
www.hostelneworleans.com
www.mardigrasneworleans.com
www.neworleans.com
www.neworleanscvb.com
www.neworleans-louisiana.com
www.neworleansonline.com
www.nola.com

## New York
www.esbnyc.com www.iloveny.com
www.hostelnewyork.com
www.letsgo.com/NYC/01-
DiscoverNYC-5
www.metmuseum.org
www.nyctourist.com
www.nycvisit.com/home/index.cfm
www.nytimes.com/top/features/tra
vel/destinations/unitedstates/newy
ork/newyorkcity/index.html
www.ny.com
www.nyny.com

## News
www.newsworks.com
www.thepaperboy.com

## Night life
www.citysearch.com
www.clubplanet.com
www.clubsindex.com
www.whatsonwhen.com/pages/
usa.jml

## Organised schemes
www.aifs.com
www.agriventure.com
www.allianceabroad.com
www.bluedogadventures.com
www.bunac.org
www.campamerica.co.uk
www.councilexchanges.org
www.earthwatch.org
www.gap.org.uk
www.iaeste.org

# web directory

www.internshipusa.org
www.resortamerica.co.uk
www.trekamerica.com
www.usa-by-rail.com
www.workandtravelusa.net
www.world-challenge.co.uk

## Philadelphia
www.gophila.com - city guide
www.phila.gov
www.philadelphia.com
www.phillyzoo.org
www.planetware.com/trees/US/PA/
PHILA.HTM

## Phoenix
www.allaboutphoenix.com
www.arizonatourism.com
www.digitalcity.com/phoenix
www.phoenixcvb.com
http://phoenix.gov
www.phoenix.worldweb.com

## Portland
http://alt.portland.or.us/index.sht
ml
http://gorp.com/gorp/location/or/
ru_port.htm
www.portlandonline.com
http://portland-oregon.com
www.pova.com

## Rail
www.amtrak.com
www.railtravelcenter.com
www.usa-by-rail.com

## Raleigh
www.raleigh.com
www.raleighcvb.org
www.raleigh-nc.org
www.raleigh.worldweb.com
www.virtualraleigh.com

## San Diego
www.gaslamp.org
www.localwally.com
www.sandiego.org
www.sandiego.cc
www.sandiego-travel.com
www.touringus.com/sandiego

## San Francisco
www.letsgo.com/SF/01-
DiscoverSF-5
www.sanfrancisco.com
www.sanfranciscoonline.com
http://sf.flavorpill.net/mailer/issue
62/index.html
www.sfvisitor.org
www.sfweekly.com

## Seattle
www.cityofseattle.net
www.kasbah.com/guides/seattle_
editorial.htm
www.pubclub.com/pacificnw/
seattlepre.htm
www.seeseattle.org
www.seattle.com
www.usatourist.com/english/places
/washington/seattle.html

## Ski resorts
www.alyeskaresort.com
www.aspenalive.com
www.aspensnowmass.com
www.bigmtn.com
http://breckenridge.snow.com
www.chestnutmtn.com
www.goremountain.com
www.hiddenvalleyski.com
www.huntermtn.com
http://keystone.snow.com
www.killington.com
www.kissing-bridge.com
www.mammothmountain.com
www.mtrose.com
www.parkcitymountain.com
www.ragged-mt.com

# web directory

www.redlodgemountain.com
www.royalgorge.com
www.shredthemoose.com
www.sierratahoe.com
www.skiburke.com
www.skidiscovery.com
www.skisnowcreek.com
www.skisnowstar.com
www.skisolitude.com
www.skithebeav.com
www.skiwisp.com
www.vailalive.com
http://vail.snow.com
www.waterville.com
www.wolfcreekski.com

## Ski work

www.coolworks.com
www.crystalholidays.co.uk
www.esprit-holidays.co.uk
www.first-choice.com
www.freeradicals.co.uk
www.goski.com
www.goski.com/usa.htm
www.inghams.co.uk
www.skiworld.ltd.uk

## St Louis

www.explorestlouis.com
www.hellosaintlouis.com
http://stlouis.missouri.org
www.stlouis.com
www.stl-music.com
www.stlouisarch.com
www.thecommonspace.org

## Tourist information

www.citysearch.com
www.routesinternational.com
www.travelguides.com
www.travelnotes.org
www.usatourist.com
Alabama - www.touralabama.org
Alaska - www.travelalaska.com
Arizona - www.carisona.com
Arkansas - www.state.ar.us

California - www.gocalif.ca.gov
Colorado - www.colorado.com
Connecticut -
www.tourism.state.ct.us
Delaware - www.state.de.us
Florida - www.florida.com
Georgia - www.gomm.com
Hawaii - www.hawaiiguide.com
Idaho - www.visitid.org
Illinois - www.enjoyillinois.com
Indiana - www.enjoyindiana.com
Iowa - www.traveliowa.com
Kansas - www.kansas-travel.com
Kentucky - www.kytourism.com
Louisiana -
www.louisianatravel.com
Maine - www.visitmaine.com
Maryland - www.mdisfun.org
Massachusetts -
www.mass-vacation.com
Michigan - www.michigan.org
Minnesota - www.exploreminesota.com
Mississippi -
www.visitmississippi.org
Missouri -
www.missouritourism.org
Nebraska - www.visitnebraska.org
Nevada - www.travelnevada.com
New Hampshire - www.visitnh.gov
New Jersey -
www.state.nj.us/travel/
New Montana - www.visitmt.com
New Mexico - www.newmexico.org
New York -
www.iloveny.state.ny.us
North Carolina - www.visitnc.com
North Dakota -
www.ndtourism.com
Ohio - www.ohiotourism.com
Oklahoma - www.travelok.com
Oregon - www.traveloregon.com
Pennsylvania - www.pavisnet.com
Rhode Island -
www.visitrhodeisland.com
South Carolina - www.travelsc.com
South Dakota - www.travelsd.com

Tennessee -
www.gotennessee.com
Texas - www.tourtexas.com
Utah - www.state.ut.us
Vermont - www.visit-vermont.com
Virginia - www.virginia.org
Washington - www.tourism.wa.gov
Washington DC - www.dchome-page.net
West Virginia -
www.state.wv.us/tourism
Wisconsin -
www.tourism.state.wi.us
Wyoming - www.state.wy.us

## Tours & trips

www.adventureplanet.com
www.americanadventures.com
www.aqua-adventures.com
www.btcv.org
www.denalitrekking.com
www.earthisyours.com
www.earthwatch.org
www.echotrips.com
www.ecosafari.com
www.escapeadventures.com
www.exodus.co.uk
www.exploretours.com
www.exploreworldwide.com
www.farflung.com
www.red-jeep.com
www.rockclimbingschool.com
www.travelbag-adventures.com
www.travelpackusa.com
www.wildernesstrips.com

## Travel kit

www.catch22products.co.uk
www.travelwithcare.co.uk

## Visa information

www.britainusa.com
www.fco.gov.uk
www.unitedstatesvisas.gov
www.usais.org
www.usembassy.org.uk

## Volunteering

www.4work.com/volcenter.html
www.agriventure.com
www.amnestyusa.org
www.ciee.org
www.gap.org.uk
www.globalvlntrs.org
www.habitat.org
www.oxfamamerica.org
www.servenet.org
www.volunteeramerica.net
www.volunteermatch.org
www.volunteers.com
www.worldvision.org

## Washington DC

http://dcpages.ari.net/
www.letsgo.com/DC/01-DiscoverDC-5
www.si.edu
www.washington.org
www.washingtondc.com
www.washingtondc.worldweb.com
www.washingtonpost.com/
wp-srv/travel/visitorsguide.htm

## Weather

www.intellicast.com
www.usatoday.com/weather
www.weather.com

# backpackers diary

The backpackers diary is a template for a weekly diary so that you can record your experiences and journey during your travels. You can either photocopy the page or use the headings in your own notebook. It's in note form, so you can jot down where you have been, and what you did on a weekly basis. One of the things that makes travel so great is the people that you meet - you can use this page to make a note of people's email addresses and phone numbers while you are out and about.

There is space to record the high points of your trip (there'll be low points too but you don't want to remember those!) and to reflect on how your journey is affecting you in the "What I learnt about myself" section. Independent travel should be about taking a journey in every sense of the word - physically and mentally. When you come home you should be more mature, confident and ready to tackle all the challenges that life throws at you.

The budget section will help you keep track of how much cash you have available - we've included it because we've been there! We know what its like trying to keep track of what you are spending on credit cards, how much cash you have, how many traveller's cheques you've cashed and what its all costing you while you are travelling around or experiencing exciting new places.

So good luck on your travels, and if you have any experiences or photos you would like to share with the world, why not email them to us at...

  info@gapwork.com

And you could be featured on...

  www.gapwork.com

# date -

**Where I went:**

**What I did:**

**People I met:**

Email addresses:

Phone numbers:

**High point:**

**What I learnt about myself:**

**Budget:**

| | cash | credit card | debit card | travellers cheques |
|---|---|---|---|---|
| Accom | | | | |
| Travel | | | | |
| Food | | | | |
| Drink | | | | |
| Socialising | | | | |

# date:

**Where I went:**

**What I did:**

**People I met:**

Email addresses:

Phone numbers:

**High point:**

**What I learnt about myself:**

**Budget:**

|  | cash | credit card | debit card | travellers cheques |
|---|---|---|---|---|
| Accom |  |  |  |  |
| Travel |  |  |  |  |
| Food |  |  |  |  |
| Drink |  |  |  |  |
| Socialising |  |  |  |  |

# date:

## Where I went:

## What I did:

## People I met:

Email addresses:

Phone numbers:

## High point:

## What I learnt about myself:

## Budget:

|  | cash | credit card | debit card | travellers cheques |
|---|---|---|---|---|
| Accom | | | | |
| Travel | | | | |
| Food | | | | |
| Drink | | | | |
| Socialising | | | | |

**RESOURCES**

# my address book

usa

A

B

C

D

E

F

G

H

I

J

K

# my address book

L

M

N

O/P/Q

R

S

T

U

V

W

X/Y/Z

# personal details

**Name:**

**Home address:**

**Home telephone:**

**Email:**

**NI number:**

**Passport number:**

**Tax file number:**

**Doctor telephone:**

**Blood group:**

**Dates to remember:**

**Flight dates & times:**

# notes

# index